TALK TO THE HAND

TALK
TO THE
HAND

A FIELD GUIDE TO
PRACTICAL PALMISTRY

VERNON MAHABAL
Director of the Palmistry Institute

**WEISER
BOOKS**

This edition first published in 2018
by Weiser Books an imprint of
Red Wheel/Weiser, LLC
With offices at:
65 Parker Street, Suite 7
Newburyport, MA 01950
www.redwheelweiser.com

ISBN: 978-1-57863-613-6
Library of Congress Cataloging-in-Publication Data available upon request.

Cover design by Jim Warner
Cover art iStock.com/skeeg
Interior illustrations by Jahnava Chan-Edwards
Typeset in Dante

Printed in Canada
MAR
10 9 8 7 6 5 4 3 2 1

This book is dedicated to His Divine Grace
Srila Bhaktivedanta Narayana Maharaja.

CONTENTS

Part Three:
Tracking and Observing on the Palmistry Trail, 65

PART FOUR:
FIELD NOTES OFF THE BEATEN PATH. 151

Introduction to the Art of Palmistry

The most majestic of all Intuitive Arts is the practice of palmistry. Like a book, our palms contain the story of our life. We've all heard it said that "life does not come with instructions." It does actually—it's written on our palms!

Our palms disclose where we've been and what we are here to learn. More importantly, they reveal what we are born to do, and the love we are driven to seek. Our primeval soul resides within the center-most core of the physical heart and speaks its message through the agency of the hand. There are many forms of divination, such as astrology, numerology, and the tarot. However, the path of palmistry is most powerful because the palm's engravings are carved directly by the soul. We are "one" in spiritual assembly, but unique in our individuality. It is our oneness that seeks spiritual identification, but it is our individuality that seeks personal expression. Our enthusiasm for life manifests when we pursue our unique path. The hand speaks its own language, and *Talk to the Hand* will open the book of your life.

The entire market of hand-reading treatises is exclusively limited to "how-to" offerings. Deciphering the story within the hand depends on both labored memorization of large amounts of data and its meticulous recall. In addition, for the greatest accuracy, thousands of hand imprints must be added and subtracted, as markings are never appraised in isolation. As a result, individuals who have a specific or time-sensitive inquiry are unfortunately obliged to plow through an entire course for relevant insight. Moreover, although hundreds of palmistry books have appeared over the last forty years, I would not recommend more than ten of them. The issue is that hand readers unindustriously employ a speculative out-of-date *deductive* system, rather than an astrologically sound *inductive* one. Though planetary terminology abounds in the field, the lion's share of palmists are surprisingly unconversant with basic astrology. Unless and until hand readers approach the palm as an actual zodiacal chart (and know how to properly read it as such), the hand's contents will always remain under lock and key.

In the course of their study, accomplished hand analysts expertly and simultaneously employ two contrasting techniques: analytic zodiacal assessment and complemental psychic reception. I will discuss this fascinating and enchanting palmistry pathway throughout this book. The purpose of *Talk to the Hand* is not to employ the microscope of detail and delineation, but the wider lens of perception and panorama. In Part One, "An Insider's Guide to Palmistry," I will share my personal experiences as a reader of hands, and through this discussion, you will learn the deeper considerations that go into astrological augury. I will also share with you the questions I have been most frequently asked throughout my career, with the aim to provide stark clarity and perspective into the sometimes confusing Intuitive Arts arena.

In Part Two, "Palmistry Expedition Journal," we will grab our hiking shoes and begin our journey on the palmistry trail. In Part One, we look upon the hand's philosophy, but in Part Two, we begin our actual practice. The underlying uniqueness of this part is that it specifically focuses on the individual's current psychological state of affairs. Additionally, the examples within Part Two are the easiest of all to identify because they are structural rather than "Stellar"!

Part Three is the heart of the book, and the approach I've laid out sets it far apart from other available books on palmistry. This section, which I call "Tracking and Observing on the Palmistry Trail," is your field guide to a largely unknown realm (the realm of hand reading), which is teeming with far-reaching information. With this guide, you'll be able to easily and quickly identify deep-seated qualities and abilities within others, all in order to better understand and work with your friends, lovers, family, and business associates. This guide is a "personality profiler," so use it when you require a quick personal snapshot. The more you use this quick reference guide, and the more you continue to employ this material, the more these patterns will intuitively "imprint" upon your consciousness. Should you take your studies further, you'll already be on the fast track of the inductive!

Our journey continues well into the night, as we reach our fourth and final part of this book, "Field Notes Off the Beaten Path." Darkness sometimes makes the path more difficult, so with that in mind, we will look at a few very challenging palmistry terrains.

Of course, the best and preferred introduction to palmistry is to seek out a live, personal, one-on-one consultation with a qualified reader of hands. That is why in Part One I introduce you to the full scope of the Intuitive Arts so that you are able to identify a first-class reader and receive a first-class reading. You will find that palm readers abound—anyone can hang a shingle and proclaim to be an "intuitive." The field of astrology boasts a good measure of serious and respectable practitioners, but unfortunately, the same cannot be said for the world of palmistry. Having been in the occupation for over thirty years, I reluctantly have to admit that fewer than fifty readers on this entire planet are genuinely conversant with the natural laws of scientific hand analysis. Fraudulent and mediocre readers are everywhere.

Having said that, a new breed of sincere practitioner is slowly emerging, willing to do the necessary work of deeply researching the discipline. Additionally, the public is becoming more aware and more discriminating. The eminent Dr. William Benham once said, "Palmistry is a study worthy of the best efforts of the best minds." I have written this book, therefore, to present a reliable, clear, and authoritative guide, and at the same time to advance the cause of this most dignified art.

PART ONE

An Insider's Guide to Palmistry

Palmistry is a mysterious art to most people, and as such, I am often asked a number of questions, ranging from its history to what it can reveal. In this part, I will share the most commonly asked questions and, through the answers, provide some of the hidden truths of the art.

MY PATH OF PALMISTRY

Q *What led you to become a palmist? How did you learn?*

A When I was twelve, my parents took me on a trip to Mexico. My dad took me to the Maya Pyramids (the Sun and the Moon) just outside Mexico City, and we climbed one of them. Having reached the top, I remember my feeling of amazement as I took in the view. Breathless, I took my time descending while my dad walked away quickly. When I was midway down, and still in awe, a voice, disembodied but very clear, spoke, "Don't think that your modern civilization is so advanced." And in only what I can refer to as a "download," I received, very quickly, an apperception of the exceptionalism of the Ancients. It was from that day that my deep distrust of modern academia began; I then and there was gifted with full apprehension of the scientific and philosophical superiority of our global antecessors—and at the same time made aware of the intentions of our current institutions to suppress this knowledge.

My first introduction to hand analysis began when I found a tome entitled *On Reading Palms* (by Peggy Thomson) in my high school library. Although I had no reference at the time, it had a very West Coast, New Agey feel to it. This was 1976, and I was surprised that my high school would even stock a book like this. This title and *The Jungle* by Upton Sinclair were most influential during my high school years. My father was quite intent on my attending college, but I could not be less attracted to their halls of arrogance and atheism. After half a semester at Berklee College of Music (I was a violinist), I met some very dedicated students of Eastern spirituality (specifically Gaudiya Vaisnavism) and went on to live in an ashram. I learned Sanskrit, Eastern spirituality, and Vedic cosmology. I couldn't have been more happy.

After five years of devotional practice at the ashram, I moved to Queens, New York, which led me to meet the person who would become my palmistry preceptor, Patrick Geoffrois. Patrick would give readings on a table he set up on St. Marks and 3rd. Meeting up with my friends in Manhattan's East Village, I would regularly see him give consultations. I began to realize that I was quite drawn and attracted to this theater of soothsaying. With a silver pentacle around his neck, black vest and black trousers, and long blonde hair surrounding an angular aquiline face, Patrick had the look of a sage wizard one might have encountered in medieval Europe. On this busy bohemian street in lower Manhattan, I would continue to be astonished at the extraordinary depth of insight he would provide to those he read for. Being new to the world of clairvoyancy, I was nevertheless aware that this reader of hands was a frequent traveler to the world "beyond the veil." I could tell that he genuinely knew its secrets, and I wanted to know what he knew. Interestingly, the Line of Intuition (see page 56) displayed upon Patrick's palms continues to be the most powerful specimen I've seen to this day! Patrick was a popular underground figure in Lower Manhattan, and everyone seemed to know him. People would come from all over the City to get their palms read. He was especially well known to those within the New Wave/Metal music scene, and of course the Wiccan and Pagan communities.

For five intense years, I spent what seemed like thousands of hours with him—watching and learning as he did his consulting. I would hang around him as much as I could, sometimes sitting late into the night at his St. Marks table. He was my teacher and mentor—one of the most influential people in my life. Whether he was engaged in his work, or just walking the East Side, Patrick answered my endless questions, opening my eyes to deep occult secrets. I remember almost everything Patrick told me. He taught me hand reading from the Western Mysteries tradition. My brand of palmistry is therefore more astrological, less New Agey than that of my peers. Patrick was a disciple of His Divine Grace Srila Prabhupada—the magnanimous Spiritual Guardian who brought

Patrick Geoffrois in New York City in 1986. Photo by Diane Edgerly.

the teachings of the Bhagavad Gita to the West (the Hare Krishna movement). When Srila Prabhupada left this world in 1977, Patrick returned to the Intuitive Arts, incorporating the Eastern teachings into his Western model. The Vedic ashram I previously spoke of was of the same lineage of Patrick's spirituality. Oftentimes when discoursing on palmistry or the mystical arts, he would begin by saying, "You know how Prabhupada would say in the Vedas . . . well, in Western Magick . . ." Having immersed myself in five years of training in Vedic philosophy, this type of presentation made everything very understandable.

Patrick passed away in 1992, and I continued to assimilate his teachings and build up a clientele. Desiring to also incorporate the Vedic system into my practice, I would later travel to India many times. Many palmists learn their trade in a very casual fashion, irregularly learning from books or taking classes sporadically. According to the eternal system of Jyotish (Eastern Astrology/Palmistry), formal mentorship under the auspices of an expert teacher is a requirement for the formation of a qualified diviner. The Vedic concept upholds that the relationship of student to teacher is based upon two essential foundations: rapt aural reception and dispensation of help and assistance. Practiced in tandem, the results are distinguished intuitive development.

In the West, the relationship with the palmistry instructor is one of formality and professionality. This is certainly healthy, but it does favor a more left-brained prognosticism. When one is listening to a class or receiving instruction, the emphasis within the Orient is to hear with one's heart. This approach becomes natural, as the relationship with one's teacher is more as the apprentice, less as an academic. Consequently, taking handprints, organizing the office, and bringing food and flowers are part of the training process. The teacher's expertise, wisdom, intuition, and of course, his blessings then transfer directly into the heart and mind of the dedicated student. This mystical transmutation is the very secret of the ancient occult orders. Knowledge can be attained by reason, but wisdom is attained by revelation.

Q *Does palmistry run in your family? Do you have to be born to it?*

 I've been reading hands for over thirty years. When people learn that it's actually my profession, they're intrigued. True, it's not a common or mainstream career (not yet!), but it *is* exciting and it does pay the bills. I'm frequently asked if my skill runs in the family, as palm reading is most often seen as a psychic art passed down the ancestral line. Having met hundreds of readers on my path of palmistry, I've yet to meet even one who learned from a family member and continued on to become a professional. (This *may* be the case with a tarot reader, but never a palmist.) I *have* met people who tell me they've garnered a little from their grandmother or aunt, but they're the types who are forthright about being a novice. Having said that, my experience is that there *is* certainly something about it that has the feel of destiny: You don't pick it—it picks you. I have always been extremely attracted to it and intent to learn it—but not because I wanted to make it my career. Nevertheless, palmistry became my career. This seems to be the standard scenario for all professional readers. It's not a vocation of bloodline—but of birth.

Q *Is this a gift?*

A When asked, "Is it a gift?" appreciatively, readers will attest to its holding a natural, almost mystical attraction for them. Further acknowledging that its principles are probably easier for them to assimilate than most, they will not discount the years of study and practice required for its mastery.

Every good reader has two marked passions in common: an ardent interest in human nature and an enchantment with the Stars. In fact, the best readers do not even identify much with being psychic. Actually, it's these "psychic readers" that you have to watch out for—the ones who fully promote themselves as psychic readers. I don't even consider palmistry, at its heart, to be a psychic art but an astrological one. This is not at all to dismiss its extrasensory feature—but to really be able to decode the arcane contents within the hands, one must possess firm grounding in its planetary foundations. The readers' intuitive skills then become icing on the cake, helping to reinforce their findings.

It's a rare thing to find a psychic reader who is not a fraud. Moreover, those few who are genuinely psychic are notoriously *on* with one client and *off* with another. Intuitive powers, as a rule, are intermittent—and therefore difficult to harness. The astrological hand reader will always be able to deliver an in-depth and accurate reading, even without the aid of intuition, as what the reader is truly employing is the hard science of the Zodiac. And yet, there is very much a psychic side to hand reading. After years of doing consultations, even the most scientific reader cannot help but become sensitive to the transmundane forces radiating from the hand. This is the beauty of palmistry. It cannot be discounted that those who walk the path of palmistry are far more intuitive than their astrological brethren. Therefore, reading a hand, rather than a chart, attracts them.

Interestingly, there is a third category of readers who fit somewhere between the two in proficiency—"New Age" palmists. No more than rudimentary in astrological expertise, these palmists prefer to tap into the palm's auric field. Auras are subtle frequencies that emit from the palm's chakra grid (the lines). In tandem with their intuition, these readers employ affirmations, crystals, and the occasional spirit guide for entrance into this field. Their readings focus almost entirely on emotional and psychological issues. While positive and well meaning in their approach, they are given to be overly esoteric and somewhat general in their statements. New Agers have the faith but not always the foundations—being composed of much sentiment but not enough science. Therefore, their discourses on the spiritual fail to impact the professional. Nevertheless, although their pronouncements may indeed be on the vague side, there is no question of their superiority over the psychic reader. New Agers also do not pick their path of palmistry—the path finds them. All the New Age hand readers I've ever met were the "lone spiritual wolves" of their families.

 Did you have to study it?

True palmists have a quenchless curiosity about everything "hands." Although they posses an easier grasp of the subject matter, they are nevertheless ceaseless in their desire to learn and study it. The best readers are researchers of the hand. They read everybody's books, attend all the lectures, and travel the world to uncover its knowledge. They are fascinated by what the ancients knew, as well as the exciting discoveries of today. To be truly great, readers must be familiar with everything that came before them: the various systems and their colorful proponents. Further, great readers will seek to add something to the craft for future generations. And they are constantly reading hands. Wherever they are, and in whatever situation, they are found learning and observing. The people they are reading will also hear something of themselves, and benefit. Palmistry is a fascinating art, and its knowledge is endless.

Yet, I've seen many readers over the years learn from a good teacher—only to get stuck in that teacher's system. They neglect to further their own research, failing to grow, expand, and contribute. The hand is a living astrological chart, and for both reader and client, its "product" is the advancement of consciousness. Therefore, its own practitioners should be at the highest platform of discernment and vision. Palmistry is a study worthy of the best efforts of the best minds.

 How old is palmistry? Who invented palmistry?

The advancement of consciousness, rather than the advancement of materialism, was always central for the Ancients. Consequently, the art of hand reading was societally interwoven and held in high esteem. More than five thousand years ago, teachings were received orally—from mentor to apprentice. Nothing was ever required to be written. The Ancients were *shruti-dhara* (Sanskrit)—able to easily remember all that they had heard.

Aware that the Iron Age (Kali Yuga) in which we now live would require that this knowledge be written down or be lost, the teachings of the most learned palmist, sage Garga Rishi, were gathered and compiled into a single volume, the *Hast Sumudrika Shastra*. Penned in Sanskrit and dated to 3100 BCE, it literally translates to "the divine scripture of hand analysis." To this day, it remains a treatise of great importance.

Proponents of this lineage hold that Eastern principles were never acquired by the process of trial and error, but taught ages ago to qualified students by visiting celestials. The Occidental (Western) system of palmistry more or less grew through an inductive methodology of research and investigation. Nevertheless, its better practitioners were very sincere and made much effective headway. Having said this, the last fifty years have seen the European and American palmists move to surpass their Vedic counterparts by updating the planetary positions to exacting measurements and modernizing the archaic and outmoded terminology. Further, it is seen that Western palmists are on the cutting edge of many astrological advances, with the best ones working to synthesize the two beautiful systems. Unfortunately, our experience is that our Eastern brethren have not been as excited to move their science forward—even curiously maintaining an elitist attitude.

 What is the difference between palmistry and astrology?

A "snapshot" of the exact positions of the heavenly bodies is taken the minute a child leaves her mother's womb. This photograph becomes the map of one's life destiny. With the help of good cosmological software, the modern astrologer need only type in a person's birth time and place of birth in order to pull up that significant snapshot. Studying the various planetary positions in symbolic form, the astrologer is then able to form a picture of that person's character, nature, and future.

Palmistry is *also* an astrological art. Palmistry and astrology are sister and brother to each other. The palm and fingers contain our entire zodiacal layout. What the astrologer can see in a chart, a palmist can see in a hand. All of the planets, houses, and signs are represented—even asteroids. This is well understood in Asian countries such as China, Japan, and India. In fact, astrologers in these countries will frequently glance at the client's hands to reconfirm what's in the birth chart. In the Western world, one is either a palmist *or* an astrologer, and when people learn of the connection, it's a revelation.

For the most precise reading, an astrologer requires an exact as possible birth time. An inaccuracy of as little as fifteen or twenty minutes will place the Stars in the wrong signs and houses, leaving even the best astrologer with a dissatisfied client. Hospital personnel and parents alike routinely jot down only approximate times at best. However, an accurate time is essential for an accurate reading.

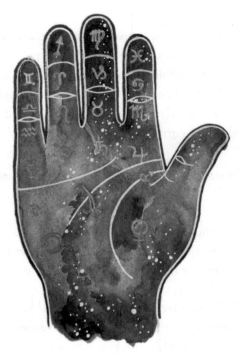

Alternatively, a hand reader does not at all require a client's place or time of birth, as the entire panorama of stars and signs is precisely engraved, visibly and concretely, into the palm. The veracity of the reading is then only dependent on the skill of the practitioner. So, although they are the same science, this is one of hand reading's great advantages.

As stated previously, palmistry is the "sister" of the two, and the reason is that its very manufacture lends itself to a more intuitive, subconscious approach. It therefore draws a more "psychologically inclined" individual than those who take to chart astrology. (Astrologers tend to be more left-brained.) This could also be a drawback if the hand reader relies too much on intuitive skills (which may be intermittent) and if the astrological data bank is also not up to speed.

Those palmists exclusively employing a purely analytical approach (astrological, sans psychic) can certainly deliver a very thorough and comprehensive consultation. At the same time, after fully assessing the zodiacal coffer, palmists may then engage intuition, reading around the planets, so to speak, powerfully enhancing and deepening the reading. This is the true beauty of hand analysis.

 Q *How much of what you do is psychic?*

A The measure of psychic faculty put to use depends on the person being read for. The more earthy the client, the more astrology can be employed. The more emotional the client, the more intuition is required. In the survey of career direction, then, readers can singularly depend on the Stars. An even mix of astrology and intuition will be applied in the arena of relationships—intimate and domestic. And for those inquiries regarding the spiritual and devotional, one's psychic talent must be summoned. Hand readers are more psychic than astrologers but less psychic than "psychics." And, other than the job description of "palmist," most would be quite comfortable in the "intuitive reader" category. Whereas pure psychic readers engage their subconscious *in toto*, the intuitive technique employs both brains simultaneously (right brain = receptive, left brain = analytical). To rely exclusively on psychic premonitions does not come without problems, as checks and cross-checks do not exist. For trustworthiness and accuracy of information, the intuitive path is safer.

A palmist gazes on all the colors in the paintbox—the planets, the signs, the fixed stars, the constellations, even a few important asteroids!—taking in how they interact and work with each other. It's a process of adding, subtracting, and harmonizing. Everything is read in relation to everything else, and no indicator, however strong, is looked at in isolation. Moreover, astrology is inherently a metaphysical science; therefore, its contemplation serves to activate the psyche, arousing the reader's insight and vision. One is thus able to read around the planets, so to speak, prodigiously deepening the consultation. Additionally, the

best readers are those who possess both the intellect to analyze the data and the sensitivity to deliver it.

The zodiacal grid lays the foundations, and the reader's insights yield the details. In other words, the planets describe the home, and intuition describes the furniture. This binary mechanism of deliberation and penetration inbuilt within hand reading is at the highest platform of psychic augury.

> *Often the hands will solve a mystery that the intellect*
> *has struggled with in vain.*
> —CARL JUNG

ABOUT OUR PALMS

The saying "Life doesn't come with instructions" is not an opinion held by palmists. The hand is like a book—the book of the soul. It's an instructional manual delineating exactly what we are born to do and what will make us happy. The book is written in "Palmese," the language of the hand. The thumb, fingers, fingerprints, lines, and structure of the palm are its living pages, and palmists literally "read" it.

The book of the hand is divided into four distinct sections: (1) one's true career calling (*dharma*); (2) one's wealth and possessions (*artha*); (3) one's individuality and self-expression (*kama*); (4) one's path of spirituality (*moksha*). Also in the table of contents are the entries of emotional relationships, past-life challenges, and health trends. The last chapter describes the masterpiece we have the potential to create and leave to the world.

It's a voluminous and detailed narrative because the human being *is* complicated, but a palmist must nonetheless unlock the soul's cipher within the span of an hour. As no two human beings are alike, no two life paths are alike. Every hand is a journal to a new journey, and the palmist travels and explores it with each client. The great saint Srila Prabhupada once said, "Impossible is a word in a fool's dictionary." Hands regularly betray that people are *much* more powerful than they think they are. The reader must pinpoint both strengths and self-imposed restrictions so that their biography becomes a triumph, not a tragedy.

 Do the lines on our palms change?

A Palm reading is often thought to be an art specific to the study of lines. These lines form an energy grid that chart the sensual, mental, and intellectual development of the human being. Classical palmists felt that an "astral fluid" of planetary origin both created and flowed throughout the lines. The palm is home to many hundreds of etchings—and of these, seven are very significant because they correspond directly to the metaphysical chakra system. Our planet Earth has its own chakra system called the ley-line grid. It is an extensive underground artery of efficacious magnetic vortexes. Previous, more advanced civilizations took advantage of the effects of this power grid by erecting cathedrals, sacred places, and pyramids upon this network. The lines on our hands are a ley-line grid system in miniature.

A few components on the palm, such as the fingerprints, never change—but the energy grid of lines is always in flux. The reason is that this grid is like a GPS system. It explains where we've been in the past, what has happened, and where we are now. In other words, lines are in real time.

Think of each crease as a flowing river. The deeper and darker the crease, the more power it carries. Like a river, a crease should look clean and clear. If so, its energy will be dynamic. Similarly, logs and branches (criss-crossing lines, indentations, and so forth) can block its

path, lessening its good effects. Nicely flowing lines show strengths and capabilities while weaker creases point out struggles and difficulties.

So, like a diagnostic test, these lines let the palmist know in real time which avenues in our life are strong (which to capitalize on) and which are weak (which to work on). If it's in our life, it's in our hands!

 Aren't the lines caused by flexing the hand?

 It is a fact that the flexing of hands does indeed fold the skin into the main lines, as they are acutely indented. However, mere flexing could not produce the hundreds of interesting patterns that the lines form into. The palm is home to a fascinating array of geometric symbols, such as stars, triangles, and circles. Not to mention the absolutely captivating designs that make up our fingerprints! In many areas in the palm, flexing is at a minimum, but the lines are at a maximum.

Observe a few dozen pairs of hands, and you'll notice an intriguing template. The upper transverse crease commences from the edge-most side of the palm (under the little finger) and finishes up near the index finger. The middle transverse crease begins from the thumb-side edge, to end an inch or so under the little finger. A mere opening and closing of the hand would simply fashion a straight-across crease from one side to the other. Instead, we notice starting points of yin / yang symmetry, which is the stuff of astro-graphy rather than the arbitrary.

The creases constructed on our palms emanate from two separate stations: the eternal soul within our heart and the zodiacal code within the brain. The soul etches the spiritual data, and the brain transmits the planetary data. As every part of us, material and spiritual, is a microcosm of the macrocosm, our celestial sky chart in miniature is etched unto our palms. "As above, so below . . ."

 Have you ever seen a hand you were unable to read?

 "I was told by a palmist that my hands are too complicated to read." An undercurrent of the unethical still persists, as remarks like this are still frequent. Producing only anxiety and confusion, such statements unmask the pretender. Sincere students will admit to what they cannot answer, but unscrupulous readers will fabricate what they don't know. As one conversant in a language can read any book in that language, one conversant with hands can read any hand. To those unacquainted, palms appear puzzling, but to those proficient, palms are prescient.

 Do you need to see both hands?

Yes. The left palm is a window to our inner self, and our right palm the outer self. The left hand is owned and operated by the right (subconscious) brain, and the right hand is directed by the left (conscious) brain. The left hand provides insight into our deepest desires and feelings, and the contents of our right hand reveal career directions and practical concerns. It's therefore imperative to study both hands for the most complete and balanced synopsis. As it's the stockroom of the inner psyche, it's commonly held that the inventory of past lifetimes is stored exclusively on the left palm. However, as our present life, inclinations, and proclivities are the result of previously performed analogous activities, the right hand also houses past life information.

 I'm left-handed—does that mean anything?

A Left-handers make up just around 15 percent of the population, and to a hand reader, a significant particularity exists. A dominant left hand literally points out that one's fundamental approach to life is chiefly right-brained. The heart rather than the intellect and the intuition rather than mundane logic direct the operations. As the right subconscious brain is connected to an empyreal expanse above the five senses, left-handers receive impressions from beyond our time and space. Throughout history and in every field, the number of inventors, pioneers, and groundbreakers who have been left-handed is inordinately higher than the 15 percent of population representation.

The inner voice of intuition is also heard by right-handers. But as their left brain is the more powerful, intuitions are checked at the door of deduction. Second-guessing their inner mystic, they surrender to the outer mundane.

Q *Can you read your own hands?*

A Good palmists can certainly read their own hands, thereby enjoying a respectable level of self-awareness. Indeed, to "know thyself" is palmistry's primary objective! In the reading of hands, two distinct theaters exist: the outer theater and the inner theater. Features such as musical, mechanistic or athletic talent, financial and organizational aptitudes, and the timing of future events belong to the outer theater. For the palmist, attributes of this type are quite easy to identify, as they deal with the practical and the utilitarian. The inner theater, by comparison, houses one's emotional, psychological, and behavioral temper. Accordingly, inter-personal relationships, social influences, and deep-rooted challenges are its main themes. Not surprisingly, this inner theater is much more difficult to apprehend, as the ability to be objective about one's own psyche drops off significantly. Even though readers may possess exceptional insight into the subjective departments of their clients, they may be no more intuitive about themselves than the next person. Make note that the scenario described here is the same for the chart astrologer.

Nevertheless, there is hope for the palmistry tribe. Intuitives also love to receive readings, and in this line of work, its almost expected that a reader will consult a peer for objective insight. How different from a mechanic who can repair their own car, or a chef who can fix their own meal! When palmists get together for coffee and conversation, it's a safe bet they will exchange consultations. And professional readers love these types of exchanges, as it gives them an excuse to talk shop, share research, and learn new techniques.

LIFE AND LONGEVITY

 I have a short life line. Does that mean I'm going to die early?

The one and only feature of palm reading that most people are familiar with is the famed life line. It's also the most misunderstood aspect of palmistry. Unfortunately, its misinterpretation is the cause of much unfounded fear. For starters, most "palmists" don't even understand this line! Classically, it's thought to be a barometer of health and longevity, but it's actually a barometer of sexual passion. Examples are shown on page 26.

A deeply carved line evidences a strong sexual drive (1)—with passions becoming weakened with a lighter tracing (2). So, as a strong specimen attests to a healthy *joie de vivre*, it's no wonder that palmistry's forbearers named it the *line of life*. Erroneously, they attributed this spirit of life to the contents of health rather than sex.

As the line speaks of sexual attraction, it attendantly articulates intimate unions. The number of major (and significant minor) relationships can be viewed from this crease. Merging branch lines reveal intimate relationships—the actual point of consolidation indicating a marriage (3). The length of courtship is represented by the length of the branch. (Lines can be "dated.") For better or for worse, a break in this life line tells of a break or ending of a relationship (4). It has nothing to do with illness or death.

The direction of this line is also commonly misreckoned; this line begins its journey from the bottom of the palm and travels upward. If the line is missing or very weak at the bottom (5), it means that the desire to establish a career before starting a family is foremost.

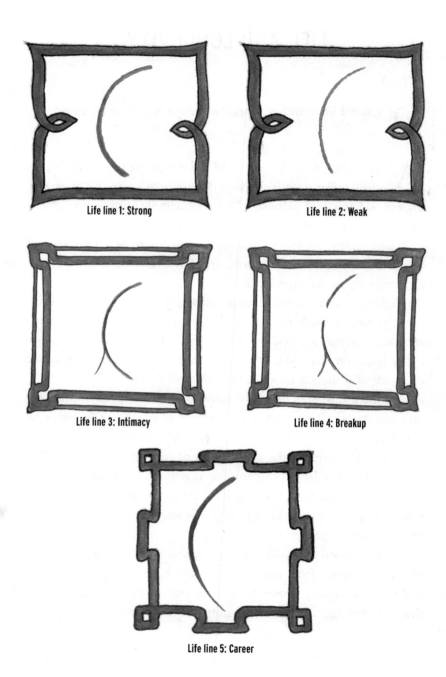

Life line 1: Strong

Life line 2: Weak

Life line 3: Intimacy

Life line 4: Breakup

Life line 5: Career

Q | Can you tell how long a person will live?

A Qualified palmists will work to address all the most important issues they find in a person's life. The goal is to provide ample insight and clarity so the best moves can be made. For most readers, psychic sight begins to wane after an hour or so. Sensing this, they will then ask clients if they have any further questions, drawing the reading to a close. And without fail, the last question is always, "Does it say how long I am going to live?"

When people think of palmistry, they usually think of "the lines." Of them, it's always the life line that's pointed out. Having the reputation for being able to determine the length of life, a break, or an ending on this line can cause some concern. This so-called life line has nothing to do with one's duration of life; it's actually the indicator of sexual relationships and sexual strength. Children are also seen from this line (and not from the area beneath the pinky finger as is so often speculated). Any merging lines, breaks, or changes on this line reveal circumstances and eventualities in love and romance, but never illness or mortality. In fact, this crease is correctly read from the bottom to the top—and palmists the world over erroneously read it from the top down. Therefore, their dire predictions are always wrong.

The hand does indeed disclose one's length of life. However, principled professionals will never include this information in their reading and are quite reluctant to make a pronouncement even if asked repeatedly. In fact, the only time readers will mention longevity is if they detect an early or untimely death, and if a possibility exists to avert it.

Personally, I think it's highly improper and unprofessional to predict one's year of death. Here's the rule: the more willing to give a date, the more a fraud. Having said this, the date of transition to one's next physical body can be ascertained by calculating the planetary transits of Saturn. Only one who is a true astrological palmist will be able to accurately determine this, and such a skilled palmist is very rare in this world.

Q *I have a lot of lines. Am I an old soul?*

A Often, just before a palmist begins the reading, clients will be seen to take a quick glance at their own hands—keen in anticipation of the secrets they hold. Confronted with the many mystifying configurations, they may sometimes exclaim, "I have so many lines—I hope you'll be able to read them!" I've also had not a few people over the years confide that they visited a palmist who informed them that their hands were "too complicated to read." Such pretenders do great harm to the Art, and to the inquirer.

Hands are a clarion roadmap into our mental geography. They offer a detailed panorama of our phrenic possessions and resources. Maps delineating rural type expanses look simple and uncluttered, while metropolitan areas depict a labyrinthine complexity. Most of the residents on this Earth have palms that resemble an agrarian landscape—relatively smooth and uncluttered with only three or four river-like lines. More uncommon are the urban type, in which the entire surface is a spiderweb of complicated patterns. Generally possessing one or two strong inclinations, the bearers of a "rural" palm achieve results by self-discipline, and like to focus exclusively at what they are good at. They are rarely interested in political affairs or that which does not directly affect their life. Those with the "urban" palm are endowed with multiple aptitudes, which means that many options and possibilities are available to them. They will candidly declare to the palmist that they are talented

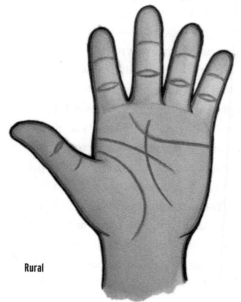

Rural

in many areas, but are unsure of which to pursue. They are enticed in various directions as their minds are alert to so much of what goes on around them. Consequently, these are the very people who will ask, "I have so many lines. Am I an old soul?"

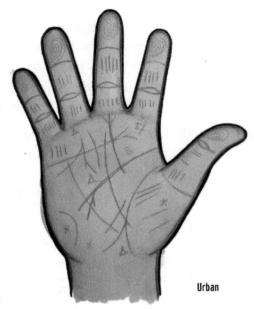

Urban

As will be outlined more clearly in the next question, transcendentally speaking, we are neither young nor old—we are eternal. Yet, from the standpoint of the metaphysical (that is, reincarnation), this concept is actually true. The rural palm evidences those souls who are relatively new to the human form (under one thousand births). Similarly, those possessing the urban palm—at least a few thousand. Volumes of collected knowledge, experience, and wisdom will be displayed on the palms of those who have inhabited a human body for millennia. Tiring of the repetition of birth and death, a discerning soul will then begin to inquire about the substantive purpose of life: self-realization.

 Is there such a thing as young or old souls?

 For seasoned palmists, the conception of "infinite consciousness" is an acknowledged reality within the course of their work. Our true authentic identity is an imperishable nucleus of individualistic singularity.

The symptom of the soul is consciousness. The symptom of consciousness is eternality. The symptom of eternality is individuality, and the most unalloyed expression of individuality is pure devotional love. Technically termed, the *jiva-atma* (Sanskrit), this antimaterial entity is suspended inside a current of flowing air within the very core of the physical heart (*prana-yoga*). It is infinitesimal and therefore cannot be seen or detected by material eyes or instruments.

> When the upper point of a hair is divided into one hundred parts, and again each of such parts is further divided into one hundred parts, each such part is the measurement of the dimension of the spirit soul.
> —*Svetasvatara Upanishad*

Interestingly, this *jiva* soul in its liberated state (free from sensual desire) is even more luminous than the Sun, but due to its extended occupation within the material world, it dims in destitution. The *jiva-atma* is not just an impersonal orb of energy, but an eternally sentient and joyful individual. We are not "one," as is now so popularly espoused, but entirely distinctive in selfhood. Though there are limitless numbers of souls inhabiting this universe, in our purified state, our relationship with the Supreme Person is intensely intimate; it can never be replaced or supplanted by another.

> *na jayate mriyate va kadacin nayam bhutva bhavita va na bhuyah ajo nityah sasvato 'yam purano na hanyate hanyamane sarire*

> For the soul there is never birth nor death. Nor, having once been, does he ever cease to be. He is unborn, eternal, ever-existing, undying and primeval. He is not slain when the body is slain.
> —*Srimad Bhagavad Gita*, Chapter 2, Verse 20

This heavyweight statement (in the ancient language of Sanskrit) was spoken to Pandava Arjuna, the mightiest warrior who ever lived, minutes before the greatest battle ever fought (the Mahabharata War). The year was 3067 BCE; the place was Kurukshetra, India; and the speaker was the Supreme Personality of Godhead, Lord Vasudeva. Witnessed and transcribed by Sanjaya the Seer, this conversation was to become the most important spiritual treatise of the East, the universally celebrated *Srimad Bhagavad Gita*.

This verse is the starting point of all spiritual knowledge, yet this cornerstone concept is almost unknown to the Occidental world. Every great advanced civilization that came before us understood this most important convention. A society conversant with this knowledge will engage in auspicious actions that will benefit rather than degrade their future lives.

Consequently, we are neither young nor old. We are eternal. Our present physical body is only a temporary "dress," and death is only a change of that dress. The body we have acquired in this lifetime was awarded to help us fulfill our desires harbored in previous lifetimes. In fact, even the personality we now identify with bears little relation to the one inherent in our constitutional state. It has been formed birth after birth, by the personages we have associated with, and the experiences we have undergone.

After many thousands of lifetimes exclusively devoted to the four pillars of animal life (eating, sleeping, procreation, and defense), a rare individual may move to become inquisitive about the actual intendment of human life: self-realization.

Therefore, clients inquiring of the palmist if they are "old souls" attest that their journey on the royal road of spiritual advancement has commenced. These are the true seekers and searchers—often feeling that they don't "belong" here. For these perspicacious souls, it is to be understood that their sojourn within this unsatisfying material sphere is now coming to a close.

FAME AND FORTUNE

 Can you tell if someone is going to be famous?

In the field of motivational self-help, it's said that the fear of public speaking is even greater than the fear of death! Quite a few occupations require one to interact with large groups of people, yet most would be quite uncomfortable having to translate what they do on camera. But there are those who live for that! And this type of fame can be predicted from the palm. We will now examine a distinct grouping that absolutely predicts public recognition.

Our ring fingers are owned and operated by the Sun, and respective of our occupational or social status, they reveal how we are seen and perceived. By studying their assemblage and the markings upon them, palmists are able to size up the particular image one presents to the world. With this is mind, it's no wonder that our brightest star is also the bestower of fame and popularity.

There are two essential components to this foreteller of fame. The first is the length of the Sun's finger (see illustrations on facing page). The second is the fingerprint. Compare the length of the Sun to the middle finger (Saturn). If the Sun reaches to the middle point of Saturn's upper segment, its length is average (1). If the Sun finger measures beyond this point (millimeters are important), it's most likely longer than the finger of Jupiter. Owners of a longer Sun are about individuality and image, while longer Jupiters are about power and influence. (Excepting an injury, fingers are always the same length on both hands.)

Very rarely, you will notice a Sun finger that rivals or is the same length as Saturn (2). This length releases the full dividends of that brilliant and magnetic planet. Like the Sun, these people will be charismatic, and command attention. Those with this towering finger are

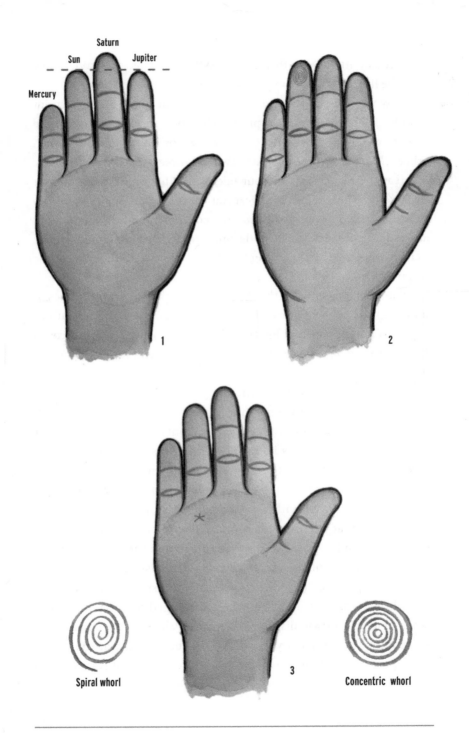

meticulously attentive to their self-expression and personal style. They crave the limelight and being center stage.

Now we come to the second component of fame: the fingerprint upon it. There are five fingerprint archetypes: the Wave (earth), the Comet (water), the Volcano (fire), the Whorl (air), and the Conch (ether). Each archetype includes two or three attendant variations. Whereas the planets identify our talents, the fingerprints outline our psychology. The exclusive fingerprint required for our purposes is the Whorl. It comes in two casts—the concentric and the spiral—and either one gains entry. Those destined to achieve substantial public acclaim will own the extra long Sun finger adorned with a concentric or spiral Whorl.

The basic objective of the Whorl print is that whatever it does, it does so in the public. For example, Jupiter is about power and authority, so a Whorl upon either Jupiter will produce the leader or the executive. Appearing on the Sun's finger, it magnifies the destiny of fame and recognition.

Vibrationally, the Whorl's circular pattern embodies the element of Air. In astrology, Air, or wind, symbolizes the qualities of self-expression and communication. Air enjoys interfacing with the other four elements, sharing its ideas. Therefore, this Sun/Whorl combo generates a person who not only attains the enlarged public arena but may also be an innovator or groundbreaker within a given field. Psychologically, those with this augur of fame have a requirement for attention that is greater than most. The reason is that the desire for applause and approval harbors deeply within their subconscious. They are consequently acutely affected by criticism and disapproval. Nevertheless, as the Sun is the source of optimism, and the Whorl— mental tenacity, they rarely remain discouraged for very long. The hands of David Bowie displayed this Sun/Whorl arrangement. Life is a continuum, so when you see this combo, know that the bearer had experience with the limelight in a previous life, still craves it, and knows how to handle it.

As a side note, examine whether you have a miniature freestanding star on the Sun's Mountain (3). If you see one, your fifteen minutes of fame is on its way!

 Can you tell if someone is going to be rich?

Financial destiny is clearly written into the hand. As there are many avenues of earning a living, the palm shows many areas of financial windows. There is not just one all-encompassing money line. Every planet, major and minor, has its own specialized career dominion. For instance, food and culinary arts are under the jurisdiction of Venus, and real estate and architecture, Saturn. So, as each parcel of the palm is ascribed to a specific planet, one's particular vein of financial achievement can be determined.

The middle transverse crease is called the seventh chakra. It speaks of our thought processes and the matters on which we focus. This crease comes in two archetypal forms: straight and curved. Logical and analytical describe the brain work of those bearing a straight crease, and imaginative and creative, a curved. Straight thinks objectively, and curved thinks subjectively. Both specimens are equally common.

Occasionally, this crease will be seen to end its journey with an upraised curve to the finger of Mercury. Mercury is the planet of commerce and communication. As this seventh chakra denotes one's mental inclinations, the result is a forthright pragmatism combined with powerful business acumen. The presence of this unique contour predicts and assures stunning monetary fortune. These individuals are shrewd and calculative; they seize at opportunities. This Mercury upturn is a sure augury that their health, domestic, and spiritual life will suffer in the pursuit of financial gain.

Now let's examine the arena of career expertise. Each finger is divided into three segments. Looking specifically at Mercury's finger, determine which segment—upper, middle, or lower—is the longest.

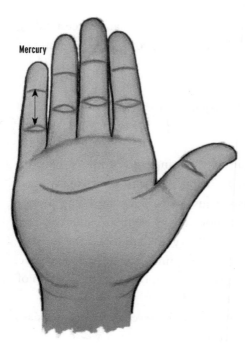

Mercury

One segment will always be longer than the other two, even if only slightly. (Do not take its width into account.) If the upper segment is the longest, these people will earn their wealth from communications. *Comedy, Singer, Writer, Speaker, Talk Show Host.* (I call this the Ozzy Osbourne combo.) If the middle segment is the longest (pictured), they will have success in the financial world. *Investments, Banking, Stock Trading, Securities, Hedge Funds.* (I call this Wall Street.) If the lower segment is the longer of the three, they will have wealth from technology. *Computers, Cell Phones, Surveillance, Electronics.* (I call this the Steve Jobs combo.)

From the standpoint of karma (action and reaction), if one was helpful and generous to others in previous lives, career success and financial reward come easily. Conversely, those who work hard at their jobs yet still struggle to make ends meet were miserly with their time, energy, and money. "As you sow, so shall you reap" is nowhere more evident than within the study of hands.

 Does my hand say if I'll win the lottery?

According to Vedic (Eastern) spirituality, this vast four-billion-mile universe that we inhabit is home to 8,400,000 species of life. It is rare, and therefore extremely fortunate, for a transmigrating soul to at long last enter into a human body. This human form of life is primarily engineered for self-realization. Consequently, we are responsible for our actions, and each and every activity we perform brings about a resultant effect—auspicious or inauspicious. In the Sanskrit language, these actions and reactions are termed *karma*. There are two divisions of karma: *sarva-karma* and *vi-karma*. Sarva-karmic activities are those that are virtuous and thereby produce happiness and advancement. Harmful actions that bring about suffering and retrogression are vi-karmic.

The palms of those who have won a lottery will evidence a previous lifetime of extensive philanthropic and humanitarian enterprises. Specifically, they benefitted their town or province in areas such as opening a hospital or an orphanage, or made it more livable by beautifying or improving it. So if they give, they must receive. As they were enormously charitable, by the subtle laws of sarva-karma, the state must return the favor in the next life. Winning a lottery will certainly produce extraordinary changes in one's life, so it *must* appear on the palm.

Enjoying a childhood with loving, well-to-do parents, having an attractive body, and receiving a good education are some of the rewards of generously sharing one's time and energy. Comparatively, those who have been unhelpful, ungenerous, or even cruel are certain to taste the same treatment from others in their next life. For example, if a child grows up with an absent father, this child was himself the absent father in a previous life. Those who are thoughtful and reflective will work to break this vi-karmic cycle, thus becoming a loving parent to their present child. It is clearly evident to a palmist that the soul is eternal, and death is just a change of "dress" (the corporeal body). By the unseen influence of nature's laws, we reap what we sow.

LOVE AND RELATIONSHIPS

Q *Is there such a thing as a soul mate?*

A Palmists are routinely (understandably) quizzed on the subject of soul mates. "Is he or she my soul mate?" "Do I have a soul mate?" "Have I met my soul mate?" "Do soul mates exist?"

We crave for that person who knows us intimately—mentally, emotionally, and sexually. That someone who brings out our best and deeply understands us—maybe even completes our sentences. And ultimately, someone whose love satisfies and completes us.

Our true self, the eternal spiritual spark, is a nucleus composed entirely of pure devotion. Therefore, we are always searching for closeness. In the Sanskrit language, this search is called *yoga*. Yoga means union. Today's popularized form of yoga is practiced primarily for improvement of physical well-being and health. However, the authentic purpose of this physical yoga is expressly for calming the mind and body. This, in order to rise above the contaminations of lust, greed, and anger. Interestingly, its execution *without* this conception at heart will actually *increase* one's material desires. To become detached from lust, and attached to love, is the prime objective of yogic practice.

Vedic literature states that the Personality of Godhead is never alone. He is always with His devotees, lovers, and admirers. He feels incomplete without them. As His parts and parcels, we are different from Him in quantity, but "one" with Him in quality. Accordingly, we don't like to be alone either! Happiness means two.

As seen from the palm, good relationships can last two or more lifetimes, and in the best cases, as many as seven. If we are in love with our partner, that love will revive in the next life, picking up where it left off. Sometimes it's seen that two people will date a few times, only to break up quickly after a small disagreement. Other times, a new couple will fight repeatedly but still go on to become an item. In the first case, a past connection had not yet formed, so a minor argument easily separates them. In the latter scenario, the two are reviving an antecedent bond, so locking of a few horns will not separate them.

As seen clearly from the hand, physical death is not the cause of relationship endings—material desires are. Two souls can never feel complete as long as an exploitive tendency exists. Intemperate degrees of lust, greed, and anger are the underlying forces behind relationship breakups. Physical appetites are illimitable and are never satiated. As seen by a palmist, relationships based on desires for sensual enjoyment, rather than spiritual advancement, are compared to two pieces of straw floating in an ocean. A wave brings them together, and they associate for some time, until the next wave separates them. The key is that if a union is based on affection rather than attachment, a relationship can last lifetimes.

 Why do we continually pick the wrong partner?

The horizontal crease, found just below the fingers, is an unsurpassed cypher for emotional compatibility. Sometimes termed the heart line (the upper thenar crease), it starts an inch below the pinky finger and makes its way toward the thumb side. This crease exhibits two very distinctive emotional archetypes, and acquaintance with their import will furnish a striking clarity. A heart line that travels a straight path throughout its entire length is the "British," and the line that ends its journey with an upraised curve is the "Italian." Emotional reserve is the predisposition of people bearing the British heart line. Even if they are emotional on the inside, they rarely share their feelings on the outside. It is challenging for them to put their feelings into words, often deflecting or changing the subject when requested. They are sometimes of the opinion that expressing their feelings is a sign of weakness. Consequently, they prefer an independent professional type who is mentally stimulating, as they enjoy discussions on finance, philosophy, and politics. They show their love by practical actions, such as making money or doing chores around the house. They live life according to how they think rather than how they feel.

Owners of the Italian heart line are quite the opposite. For their own mental equanimity, sentiments arising within their heart must find an outward expression. If their partner affords them the comfort of emotional release, growth will occur in every venture they pursue. They have strong nurturing instincts, and thrive on intimacy and closeness. Consequently, they require lots of attention and reciprocation. They live life according to how they feel rather than how they think.

British will see Italians as smothering and codependent. Italians will see British as detached and aloof.

So, to avoid constantly picking the wrong partner, look for one who has the same line as you. British should be with British, and Italian should be with Italian. Opposites attract, but they don't last. Those who have similar interests do. Partners having the same lines understand each other, allowing each to be who they naturally are.

Q *Is divorce destined?*

 If we look to the Stars for the answer to this question, we can authoritatively state that the year 1959 officially inaugurated the "age of divorce." It was at this time that the powerful planet of Uranus commenced an influential transit on the United States. Its effect was to bring forth social orders that embodied the polar qualities of those of the "greatest generation," and all those before them. Uranus is home to Indra, the mighty god of lightning and thunder. Indra is entrusted with high-level affairs of universal management, but he is also known to occasionally engage in activities that transgress the laws of nature. Like his thunderbolt, which can be destructive, the planetary progressions of Uranus will sometimes work to displace and overthrow societal order and stability.

Its appearance during the Napoleonic Era (AD 1803) began two decades of war in Europe. Its next advent in 1929 enabled a cartel of bankers to kidnap an economy and create a fiat currency. And more recently, its influence now concerns the domestic rather than the political.

In tandem with earnest spiritual and religious practice, the institution of marriage is the very foundation of a strong and sane society. From 1959 to 1999, Uranus brought in an era of unbridled abnormal sex and pornography. To destroy the institution of family, the global managers worked tirelessly to both erode traditional gender roles and promote abnormal sexuality. A population that loses its moral compass and its ability to discern right from wrong becomes weak and easily controllable slaves. The handprints of Americans born from 1810 to 1930 show that they possessed the tools required to build and maintain committed relationships. A heightened gradation of emotional maturity and responsibility is acutely visible within these old and well-worn inked prints. Uranus has since moved out of this inauspicious progression (in August 1999), and principled generations are now being born who will again restore dignity and stability to this indispensable and required institution.

LIFE AS A PROFESSIONAL PALMIST

Q *Can you make a living as a palmist?*

A Within Europe and the Orient, it's as common for people to openly remark that they have an appointment with their palmist as they would their chiropractor. In the United States, the powerful and influential regularly consult with intuitives—it's just kept very hush-hush. When it came to the attention of the media that Ronald and Nancy Reagan retained a personal astrologer (Joan Quigley), the American public was quite surprised, but to the astrological community, the response was, "What else is new?"

As the ascendancies and declines of a human being can be calculated astrologically by way of a birth date and time, so also can a new product or a commodity. When launching a new line, transitioning their marketing, or hiring a new executive, the world's largest and most successful firms consult with those who are familiar with the Stars. Major corporations have their own teams of astrologers, and when a new product is ready for market, a day will be determined when the planets are in the best positions to foment its advance. This corporate/ metaphysical merger is a mainstream practice of which the general public is wholly unaware. Although it may appear that the practice of Intuitive Arts is represented only at psychic fairs or New Age stores (or psychic reader storefronts!), the fact is that within the media, commerce, entertainment, even politics, there exists an entire world of "suit and tie" readers behind the scenes, advising those who are at the very top. J. P. Morgan once said, "Millionaires don't use astrology; billionaires do."

Times of prosperity and struggle for a nation or a republic can also be ascertained by its birth chart. In fact, it was on the well-studied commissioned advice of a secret astrological order that our founding fathers waited almost a full month to sign an *already completed* Declaration of Independence (August 2, 1776, at 5:10 p.m.). To a reader, the fact that our country grew to become the greatest nation on Earth attests to the proficiency of those forebearer diviners. (Benjamin Franklin was himself an accomplished astrologer.) Witnessing repeated templates in the thousands of hands they see, palmists can also make accurate predictions on current political, economic, and societal affairs.

Many readers begin their careers on the psychic fair circuit, and it's a great avenue in which to cut their intuitive teeth. During the course of a "professional" consultation, the palmist is expected and required to go very deep into the career and domestic affairs of the client. People are often in crisis mode when they call a palmist and seek straightforward unvarnished answers. Appointment-only readings are cordial, but the consultation itself will be earnest and no-nonsense. Not so at the psychic fair! Kiosks of crystals, books, ritual items, and clothes abound, but the main draw are the palmists, card readers, and psychics. A good share of the patrons are pagans, wiccans, and New Age seekers. Usually in good spirits, they are looking for uplifting insight and inspiration. Consultations are timed for fifteen minutes, so a reader may be able to survey as many as ten pairs of hands in the course of an afternoon. Most attendees are not too demanding in what they expect to hear and tend to weigh in on the positive, if not naïve, side. This works very much in the favor of up-and-coming readers, as patrons are not looking for specific information as much as for positive inspiration. Therefore, readers can get away with not having to be so accurate and precise. But you have to start somewhere—so if a reader is regularly participating in these public events and at the same time under the tutelage of an experienced teacher, a firm metaphysical foundation is sure to be established.

In the course of reading at parties, crystal stores, and other events (which are the first rung on the intuitive food chain), good readers will start to build up their own independent following. And those clients will in turn refer their friends—and referrals are an important share of a reader's business. If one is actually meant to do this work, clients will flock to that reader. The best readers *never* advertise or do much of anything to promote themselves. A long practicing hand reader can earn a very comfortable living by way of radio and Internet interviews, book sales, workshops, and, of course, private readings. As with other professions, readers come to be recognized for their own focus of specialization, such as financial forecasting, relationship counseling, or health insights—attracting a clientele accordingly. On any given day, there may be a teaching engagement, a consultation or two, readings at a social affair, or a talk show appearance. Travel, varied environments, and meeting the "cutting edge" is concomitant to their work. Attention and popularity also follow palmists. People are immediately curious, ask lots of questions, and quickly offer their hands for inspection. Those who walk the path of palmistry have the freedom to create their own career and enjoy their own autonomy.

A defining characteristic of most intuitives is that they easily tune into the subtle energies of those around them and the places they are in. Like an antenna, they are sensitive and receptive, which certainly works in their favor if they are hand readers. But intuitives are also known to be impractical and ungrounded, which certainly affects their ability to make a living at this profession!

Up until about five hundred years ago, palmists and intuitives were "court astrologers," valued advisers to the king, queen, and other royalty. In this day and age, however, adept intuitives are required to be possessed of a self-motivated entrepreneurial spirit. And many are! The palmist's raison d'être is the transparent intermediary between Heaven and Earth. Those who are able to synthesize and harmonize these two very polar opposites—the material and the spiritual—are the most powerful psychic agents.

At the same time, every palmist and astrologer, no matter how successful and integrated within society, has a sense of being "outside of

it" as well. That's probably how it's meant to be—as the tribal shaman traditionally lived on the outskirts of the village. This places one in the most advantageous position for objective observation. Throughout the last three hundred years, hand readers have also been portrayed as colorful, independent, or even eccentric characters—and this may be one of the keys to their survival and success.

Q *Do you tell someone if you see something bad in the hand?*

A This question is almost always asked in reference to accidents, diseases, and death. When the reader examines a pair of hands, one's entire life is illustrated. Therefore, both the positive (marriage, promotions, childbirth) and the difficult are on display. Most of our life, however, revolves around our regular everyday routine—and this is where I actually see the *bad*. As seen in 95 percent of hands, most people are in the wrong job, the wrong relationship, and in the wrong locale. A society cannot be healthy and functional if its people are so misaligned.

In the Orient, the study and practice of palmistry is called Jyotish—the "Science of Light." Throughout history, its practitioners were expected to be of the highest character—God-conscious, self-controlled, and humble. This included eating a vegetarian diet and having an aversion to drugs. One must live in concordance with the laws of nature in order to function as an adept and transparent reader of the Stars. Therefore, able to precisely guide and counsel, the palmist of yore was seen as a most valued member of society.

The job of a reader of hands is to ascertain a client's right livelihood: what they are born to do and their true meaningful work. Readers may address the dynamics of a present relationship or inform of a future partner. They may even alert one to a future affair that's best avoided.

Also important to look at is what in astrology is called *astrocartography*. Every component of our corporeal body is regulated by a specific astrological governance. In the same way, regions of the Earth have their own predominating influence. For instance, Manhattan Island is fully under the pull of economic Gemini; that's why it will always be the financial and banking center of the United States. Los Angeles is under the domain of Neptune, the planet of acting and motion pictures. Therefore, LA will always be the center of cinema and entertainment. Similarly, the palmist must determine the compatible astrological wavelength of both client and geography in order to fully empower the client's career and domestic endeavors.

An independently thoughtful class of specialists in the Science of Light (or Jyotish) can redirect a misguided society to functionality and sanity. And lastly, but most importantly, the palmist will inform them of psychological and emotional issues impeding their spiritual and devotional development.

 Have you ever read for someone who was possessed?

Interestingly, I have! Our eternal spiritual soul resides within the innermost core of the physical heart. Further, it is encased within two separate garments: the subtle body (mind and intelligence) and the outer corporeal body (blood, bones, and skin). The soul of a ghost is sheathed only by the subtle body but has lost its corporeal covering. A person may become a ghost on two occasions: a premature death or a suicide. In accordance with the undertakings performed in previous lifetimes, one is subsequently awarded a fixed life span. If someone takes their life or dies before their appointed time (vehicular accident, explosion, or death on the battlefield), that person must continue to dwell on this Earth until their destined term.

The desire to enjoy physical pleasures nonetheless continues, so the ghost endeavors to find a living body in which to inhabit. Disembodied spirits are able to inhabit those whose mind and intelligence have been weakened by alcohol, drug, or ritual abuse. The presence of a ghost can be detected when a person talks or acts uncontrollably, or is in possession of powers beyond their capacity. Recurrent or continual occupancy is clearly made evident by an off-color, ashy-gray patching on the Mount of the Moon. The Moon represents the invisible subtle mind, and the subtle body of the ghost shows up quite

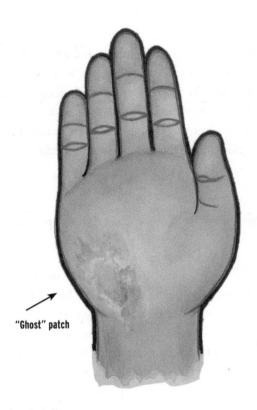

 "Ghost" patch

subtly on the hand. (In astrology, the Moon represents the mind, ghosts, and psychological invariance.)

Q *Do you believe in God?*

> *In want of other proofs, the human thumb would convince me of the existence of God.* —Isaac Newton

A The hand is a masterwork of Divine majestic design. The more one unlocks its codes, the more one beholds its intricacy and ingenuity. Suffused in physical form, it's a magnificent textbook of one's sensual, mental, and intellectual temper. Its various chapters (the fingers, the thumb, the lines, and so forth) yield beautific clarity into every area of life. The dignified philosophers of yore—Plato, Brahe, Pythagorus, Da Vinci—were strong advocates of hand reading, regarding it as a tool, given by God, for self-realization. These were the true scientists, possessed not only of great intelligence, but of great humility—quite unlike the disingenuous class of today's so-called academics.

> *The most beautiful system of the Sun, planets, and comets*
> *could only proceed from the council and dominion of*
> *an intelligent and powerful Being.*
> —ISAAC NEWTON

Faith without Science is sentiment. Science without Faith is mental speculation.

PART TWO

Palmistry Expedition Journal

alk to the Hand is a guide that will enable you to easily identify essential qualities and characteristics in yourself and in others so that you better understand and work with family, friends, lovers, and business associates.

Within the context of a complete palmistry consultation, numerous features and elements are taken into consideration simultaneously and analyzed in relation to each other. The interpretations in this section focus on specific features in isolation in order to provide a quick guide to personality traits; nevertheless, their meanings stand firm and are not diminished by supplementary or contrasting influences.

While it generally takes months or even years to ascertain a person's nature, this part will assist you in immediately assessing your talents, without having to endure the lengthy study typically associated with such disciplines. You now have a tool to identify your underlying traits and motivations, which will give you a tremendous advantage in engaging how to best use your talents and enjoy your relationships. Similarly, if someone informs you that they carry a particular personality trait or possess a specific attribute, you now have an accurate and even entertaining system to verify those qualities with certainty. Most importantly, this section is designed to be fun and easy to use!

IMPACTFUL OR ARTISTIC PALMS

What motivates you more—a creative goal or the desire for power and influence? Place your hands palm down on a table. Hold your fingers close together so that no spaces show. Now, examining only your index and ring fingers, compare their length. Which of the two is longer? (It will be the same on both hands.) The index symbolizes the desire for power and independence. The ring attends to interests of self-expression and public recognition.

IMPACTFUL

If your index finger is slightly longer than your ring finger, financial growth is very important to you. You may also enjoy having a position of management or authority. If your index seems to almost rival the middle finger in length, your requirement is to be independent and have autonomy. You would be happiest being your own boss or running your own business. In addition, a spirit of philanthropy is a built-in trait, as humanitarian Jupiter holds title to this finger. The more successful you become, the more you will share your energy and money.

ARTISTIC

If your ring finger is slightly longer than your Index finger, a creative purpose is more important to you than occupying a position of power. Those who seek careers in web design, architecture, and film have a longer ring finger and wish to attain success through an artistic pursuit. The longer index will usually go after what makes them money, but a long ring will be driven by that which expresses their individuality.

A fervent desire for public approval and recognition is found on those whose ring is almost as long as the middle finger. This is common on most successful actors and musicians. The ring finger is under the jurisdiction of the radiant Sun, so this long length bestows a natural charisma and magnetism. I often tell my students that musicians have the longer ring and their lawyers have the longer index!

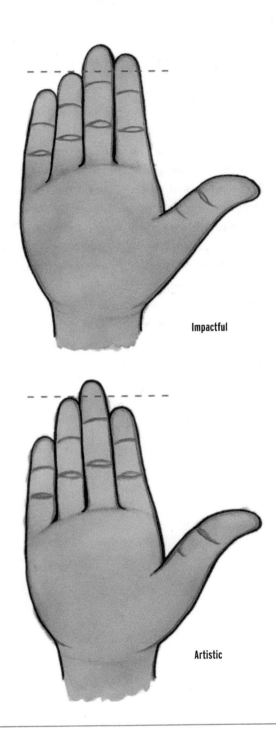

Impactful

Artistic

THE LINE OF INTUITION

This semicircular line, situated on the pinky side of the palm, is called the Line of Intuition. A rare crease, its presence announces that one's subconscious mind is active and available to be accessed. A line as deeply etched and defined as the one pictured will provide the bearer with substantial powers of psychic intuition. Inventors, intuitives, and healers of every description possess this crease.

The line pictured is a textbook specimen: deeply cut, half-Moon curvature, and integral in length. A commanding crease like this furnishes powerful clairvoyant perception and the gift of second sight.

Having said this, if your palm displays some light tracings in this area, or a few unconnected embryonic fragments, this is a clear signpost of your developing inner vision. Take a class in dreamwork, work with a pack of tarot cards, or experiment with a pendulum. As your psychic perceptions grow, you will see this line become more prominent on your palm.

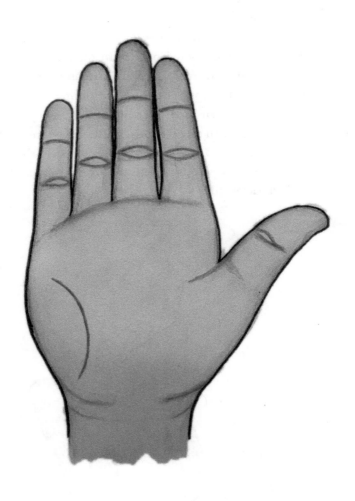

GOSSIPY HANDS

Is it possible to know if the secrets you share with your friends are safe with them? And is there a way to know if a person is a gossip? The answer is yes, and it's easy to spot. Rooted in the palm, our four fingers are astrological antennae, constantly receiving and broadcasting information.

Fingers that are held out and extended during conversation are quite spontaneous in their reception and delivery. They love to talk, and are free and easy with their knowledge. Rarely interested in political affairs, they are instead fans of everything "he said—she said." The great Joan Rivers possessed this contour in the extreme. Her fingers actually arched backward!

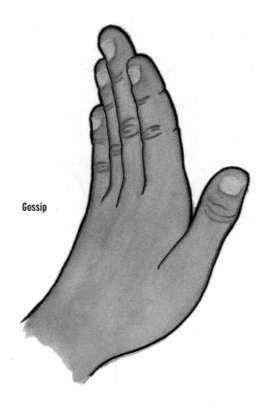

Gossip

Fingers that consistently assume a slight inner curl spend extra time listening, taking notes, and processing all that they hear. However, they are not so readily inclined to divulge what they know. Interestingly, they are very drawn to keeping abreast of national, political, and societal affairs.

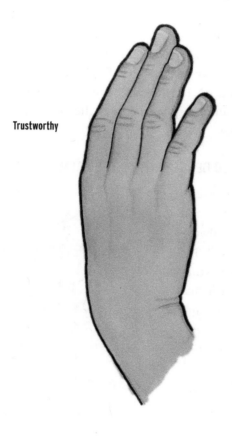

Trustworthy

SUCCESSFUL HANDS

Can you tell if someone is successful by looking at their hands? Yes, and for that, we look to the thumb. To a palmist, the most important department of the hand is the thumb. It's the only part of the hand that is not under a planetary jurisdiction (Karma). It represents personal determination and free will, and therefore the ability to shape our environment. The thumb is the gauge to let you know if you are utilizing your God-given talents.

Relax your hands by shaking them. Now place them palm down on a table. Now look at your thumbs. How far apart do they stick out from your palms and fingers? The human being has an opposable thumb, and the more the thumb opposes the palm, the more influence we have over our environment.

THUMB ANGLE AT 90 DEGREES FROM THE PALM

This placement reveals that you are a doer and a manifester. You always have big plans—and it's by taking big risks that you achieve them. You like depending on yourself and making your own decisions. You also enjoy taking charge of others. Additionally, this placement reveals a very marked level of self-confidence.

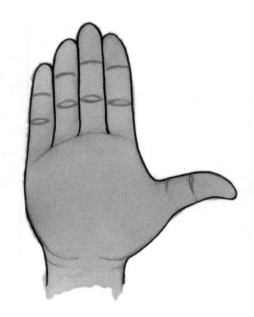

THUMB PLACEMENT AT 45 DEGREES

This placement shows an above-average ability to get your way in the world. You enjoy the process of working with a team, but you also insist on maintaining some independence. In business dealings, you strive for and achieve steady results due to a good balance between caution and impulse. You are imbued with an adequate supply of self-confidence.

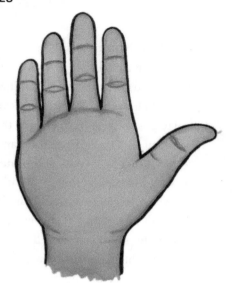

15–20 DEGREE ANGLE (OR LESS) FROM PALM

This placement discloses that you are barely applying your talents and abilities. A thumb "nesting" too close to the palm evidences much dependence on others and an underlying fear of failure. You lack strength of willpower and determination. A course with a motivational teacher can empower your resolve.

(*Note that these thumb placements are also easy to spot when people-watching.*)

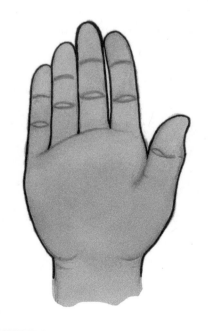

LYING HANDS

A person's character and nature are etched upon the palms—and there is a surefire signal that reveals if one is being dishonest. If a person is lying to you, and they *know* that they are lying, their ring finger will dip slightly below the other three as they speak. One or both hands will display this feature. According to the science of Ayurveda (the Oriental system of health and healing), an energy meridian originating from the physical heart emits a continual current to this finger. Based on this very intimate connection with the heart, the person's dishonesty causes the finger to retract from inner shame. The heart knows the truth and lowers this finger in guilt and embarrassment. This lowering may be slight, but it will be noticeable. Switch on a political talk show or a liberal media outlet and mute the sound. As you observe hands being waved and gestured, you'll be absolutely amazed at how frequently you see this.

Note that lying when joking or being light-hearted will never cause this occurrence. One must be deliberately obfuscating the truth in order for this finger to decline.

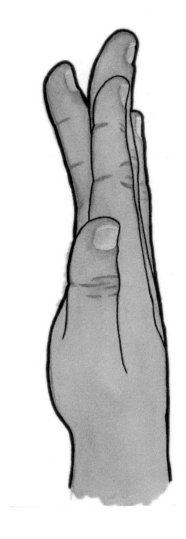

PART THREE

Tracking and Observing on the Palmistry Trail

Palmistry is an ancient science, and an unsurpassed tool for character and emotional analysis. The palmar surface of the human hand, by its very nature, contains vast amounts of detailed personal information. On this particular trail we will survey the varied topography of human nature and character. Responsible and serious practitioners have published numerous palmistry books over the past century regarding the following study; however, these texts no longer adequately address today's audience.

This part is a powerful reference and resource guide for those who want a quick and accurate way to assess their (and their partner's) talents, psychology, and emotional personality. You need not have an interest in palmistry to use this section. The diagrams and accompanying texts are deliberately simple and straightforward, providing quick access to vital answers and pressing questions. The information found here is based on extensive research and years of practice working with thousands of people. Although it has not been written with the intention of producing a professional palmist, an experienced hand reader will nonetheless find much advanced and interesting material to add to their study.

THE DIFFERENCE BETWEEN THE HANDS

The left, or objective, brain transmits its portfolio and recorded information to the right hand. The right, or subjective, brain transmits its dossier to the left hand. Therefore, the general rule is that the right hand symbolizes the outer (or rational) self while the left hand symbolizes the inner (or emotional) self. This holds true for left-handers also.

When you examine a pair of hands, concentrate primarily on the right hand, as this will chronicle the actual reality and present state of affairs within a person's life. The left hand, correspondingly, will show potentials, and what is internally wished for and desired. Comparing both hands together will give you the most comprehensive indicator of how a person will act—and interact.

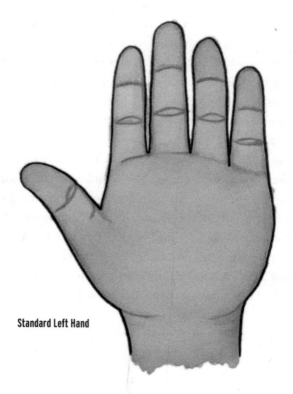

Standard Left Hand

HOW TO USE "TRACK AND OBSERVE"

Let's say you want to know if you (or your partner) is a good listener. Look up these words in the contents, turn to the corresponding page, and view the diagram. The diagram will reveal the strongest sign of listening skills found in the hand. Some entries will include an illustrative idea that I've encountered on my path of palmistry. This will add to your understanding of the character trait.

Now observe both of your (or your partner's) hands in order to see if either hand contains the configuration. A match will indicate that good listening skills are a strong talent, and they can be used effectively. Keep in mind that whenever a match occurs, the quality indicated by that specific configuration can or will play an evident role in your life.

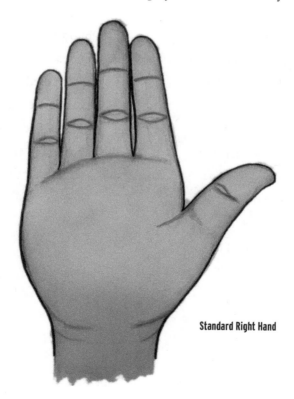

Standard Right Hand

TRAITS REVEALED

MASTER KEY OF THE HAND

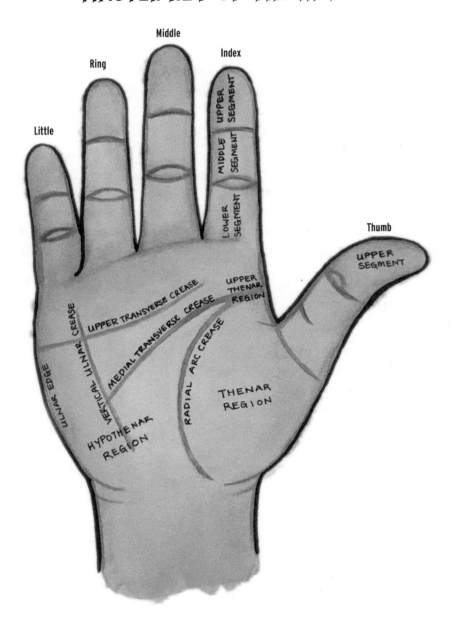

ADVENTUROUS

A person who craves physical adventure will have a hand in which the bottom of the palm is wider and broader than the top (where it meets the fingers). Notice also that the bottom edges will be thick and fleshy—and most often rounded.

CHARACTERISTICS

This is the hand found on the archaeologist, park ranger, and firefighter. It shows a need for stimulation, exploration, and physical challenges—preferably in the great outdoors. These are busy, energetic people who love their freedom. Nearly half of those demonstrating this shape of hand have the potential to be good leaders. This is a configuration ill-suited for a desk job.

QUALITIES

- Exploratory
- Outdoors person
- Restless
- Easily bored
- Likes to travel

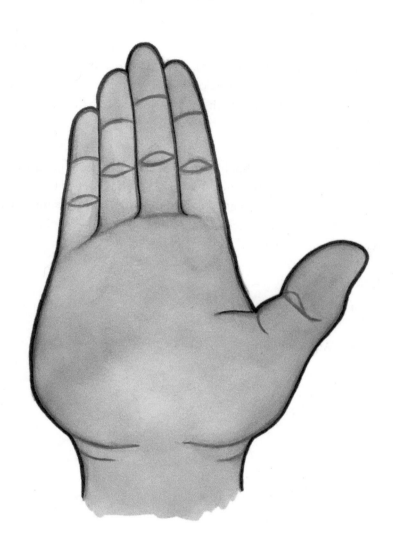

AGGRESSIVE

Examine the upper thenar region—the pad of flesh directly above the ball of the thumb. An inclination toward aggression and contentiousness is revealed by an upraised or firm development. A slightly reddish hue upon this region will both confirm and exacerbate this demeanor.

CHARACTERISTICS

These people are the bold go-getters who take the initiative to get things done. In a relationship, they may have a tendency to be forceful or obstinate. They can be good companions to those of a similar nature who can reflect their forceful nature back at them—helping them to recognize and temper it.

QUALITIES

- Bold
- Potential for anger
- Argumentative

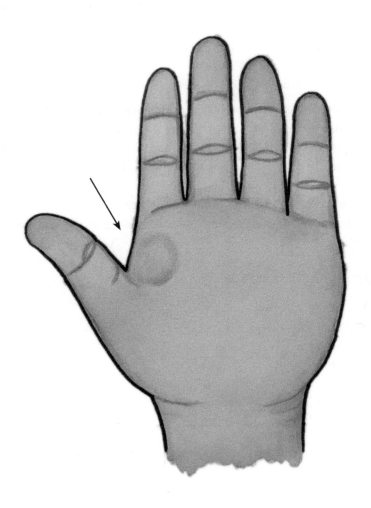

AMBITIOUS

Ambitious individuals are revealed by an index finger that has its middle segment as the longest of the three. This quality is even further accentuated if the segment is engraved with vertical lines.

CHARACTERISTICS

These people are highly motivated and very self-assertive. The index finger is the domain of Jupiter, planet of growth, furtherance, and abundance. Long middles are always planning how to move forward in their endeavors, and they pride themselves in thinking "big." As they are *take-charge* people, they require their own autonomy—even if they work for others. An optimistic and helpful nature is built into this segment, and as they become more successful, they become more philanthropic.

QUALITIES

- ⟨ Entrepreneurial
- ⟨ Self-motivated
- ⟨ Achiever

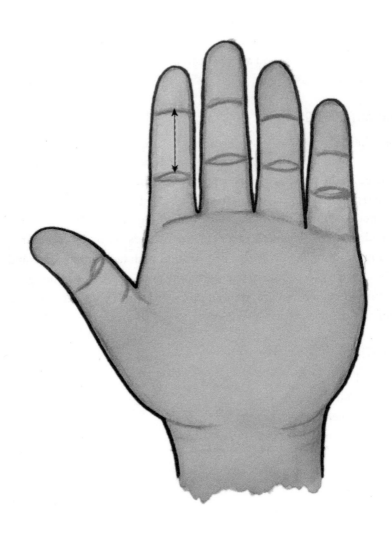

ANALYTICAL

Sometimes the medial transverse is carved "ruler straight" into the palm. These people are left-brained thinkers. Logic and reason determine their viewpoints and approach to life. In addition, straight medials excel at multitasking.

CHARACTERISTICS

"Just the facts, ma'am" is the motto for those with this analytical imprint. Their conclusions are based on hard data and statistics, as opposed to the more subjective approach of their more curved medial counterparts. They sometimes consider reading fiction a waste of time because they like to take away something that can be practically applied. Whatever their chosen field, their minds are built for research and investigation. They love to play around with facts and figures, and their solutions to problems are based on pure objective thinking. In the emotional department, they run the danger of appearing cool and aloof to their friends and loved ones.

QUALITIES

- Logical
- Calculating
- Objective
- Rational

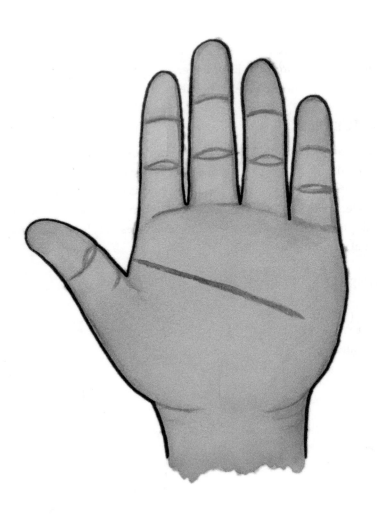

COMMUNICATIVE

The eagerness and the capability to communicate effectively are confirmed by the presence of the vertical ulna crease. (It is positioned on the palm directly below the little finger.) The line indicates a strong inclination to express one's ideas and views.

CHARACTERISTICS

A crease that is clear and clean will impart a good measure of confidence, creativity, and self-expression. Both the desire and the ability to write are also concomitant with this feature. This crease does not have to be as deeply cut as the other lines on the hand in order to bestow its good qualities. A deeply cut vertical ulna gives very powerful and influential communicative skills.

QUALITIES

- ☾ Talkative
- ☾ Expressive
- ☾ Interactive
- ☾ Effective communicator

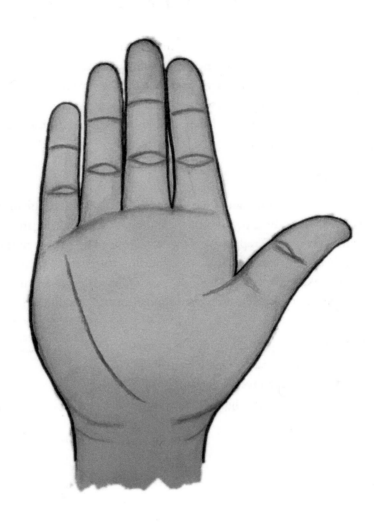

COOKING ABILITY

"If it's big in your hand, it's big in your life." The lower segment of the index finger is the storehouse of culinary arts. If it's the widest and thickest of all the other twelve, cooking ability is a major interest and talent. In addition, if this segment is also the longest of its two other brethren, these people will be quite knowledgeable in their field and may wish to teach it.

CHARACTERISTICS

I call this area "Wolfgang Puck." The wider this section, the more passion for food. These people enjoy creating tasteful and elegant preparations, and much happiness is derived from feeding people to their full satisfaction. A few strong vertical lines on this area confirm the ability to make cooking their living. Concordant with this segment's build comes the predisposition to overindulgence and weight gain.

QUALITIES

- (Loves to sample new recipes
- (Culinary inventiveness
- ("Restaurant highlighted" vacations

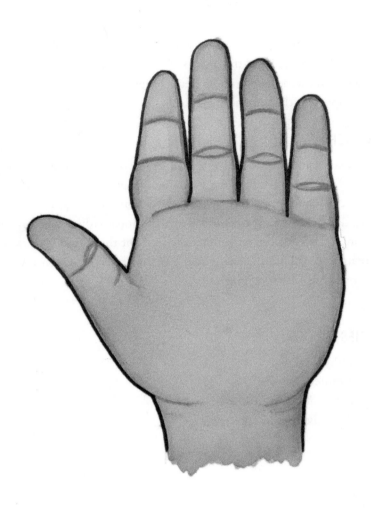

CREATIVE

Observing the palm side of the hand, compare the length of the ring finger with the index. Hold the fingers close together so that no spaces show between them. If the ring finger is longer, creative achievement is more important than financial gain.

CHARACTERISTICS

Self-expression and individualism are the realm of the ring finger, and power and influence are the domain of the index. Positions of power and leadership do not interest owners of the long ring finger. Rather, they are drawn to the creative urges and passions within their heart. They can and do achieve enormous success, but they want it by way of a creative contribution. Having said this, they often get taken advantage of by those with long indices.

QUALITIES

- ❨ Individuality
- ❨ Aesthetic sense
- ❨ Sense of beauty and style
- ❨ Attentiveness to appearance

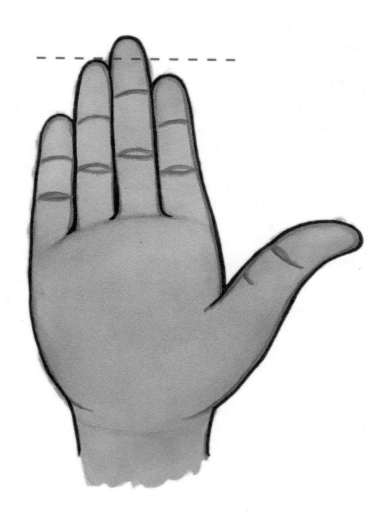

DECISION MAKER

Sometimes the medial transverse crease ends its journey within ring finger territory. This is the badge of the decision maker.

CHARACTERISTICS

These people are from New York—straightforward and direct. Problem solving and solution giving come naturally—and they trust their choices! Planning and organizing skills are in their blood, and they are often found in positions of delegation and direction. These are high-level managers, planners, and team leaders. And, as these individuals are characteristically firm, they can at times be inflexible and unable to compromise. Objectivity is not always their strongest suit.

QUALITIES

- Problem solver
- Leadership
- Coordinator

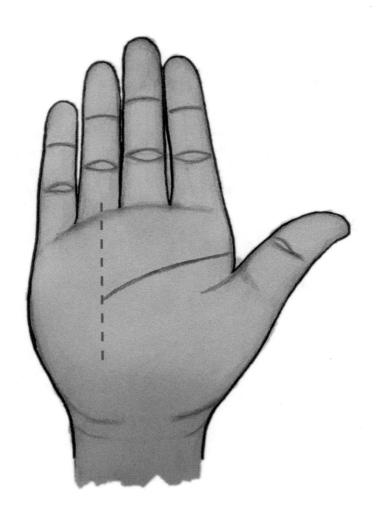

DEMONSTRATIVE

Regardless of its final destination, the ability to easily put one's feelings into words is the trademark of an upwardly curving upper transverse crease.

CHARACTERISTICS

A clear channel exists in which to express the feelings of the heart. These people make good counterparts to those who are emotionally reserved. However, if this line has a very pronounced curve, it could be too much of a good thing. The greater the curvature, the more they wear their heart on their sleeve.

QUALITIES

- Romantic
- Expressive
- Shares feelings

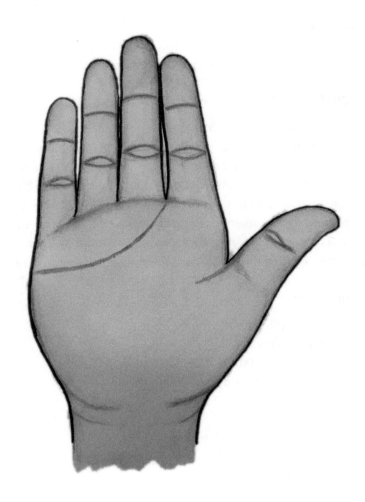

DISHONEST

From the back of the hand, take note of the shape and structure of the little finger. The greater the degree of twisting and crookedness, the greater the degree of dishonesty in communications.

CHARACTERISTICS

Those with crooked pinkies stretch or obfuscate the truth to get what they want. The danger is that they often get caught in tangles of lies or start believing their own lies. They think, "If I'm honest, I won't be as effective or have much impact. I'll be more successful if I embellish." And so they do. The highest degree of disfigurement is found on political figures, mainstream academics, and those in corporate media. Make note that the finger's structural distortions are the result of distortions within the psychology—not the other way around.

QUALITIES

- Duplicitous
- Tendency to lie
- Stretches the truth
- Untrustworthy

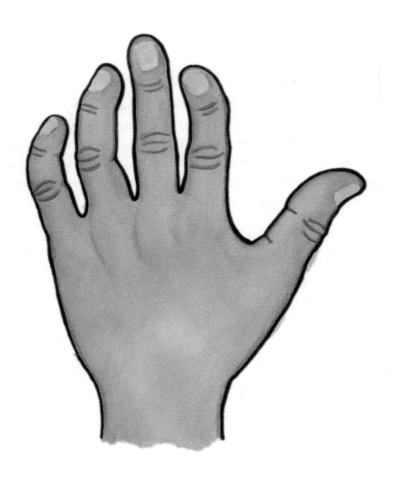

EMOTIONALLY RESERVED

The owners of an upper transverse crease that is predominantly linear—regardless of its length—are quite reserved with their feelings and emotions.

CHARACTERISTICS

Think of these people as British rather than Italian. They're not unemotional, but their struggle is to put their feelings into words. If an argument erupts, they prefer to retreat into another room to think through the situation. They require to be around loved ones who encourage them to feel comfortable in sharing their heart. Writing down their feelings is also a good therapy or outlet.

QUALITIES

- Emotionally self-contained
- Hides feelings
- Patient
- Even-keeled

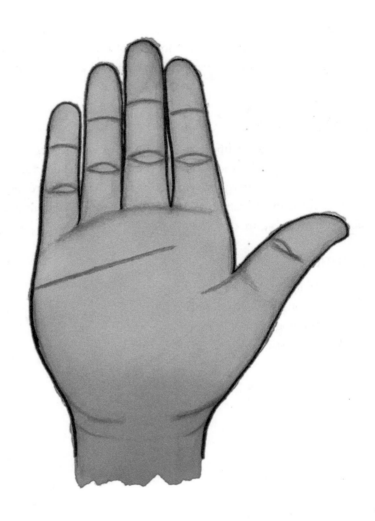

FAITH IN A HIGHER POWER

Strong belief and faith in the Supreme Person are declared when the upper segment of the index is the longest of the three. If there are vertical lines etched on it (however faint), spiritual advancement is their priority.

CHARACTERISTICS

Those with this longer upper segment have an inborn organic faith in God. They have high expectations of themselves, and any form of selfishness is anathema to them. In times of difficulty, these are the people who are most able to remain optimistic and strong. Their ultimate mission statement is pure devotional love.

QUALITIES

- Religious
- Strong values and morals
- Ideological
- Altruistic

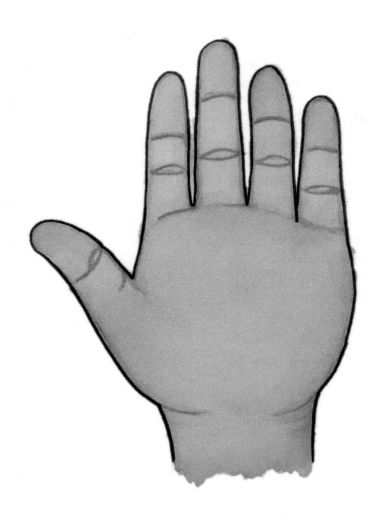

FAMILY-ORIENTED

A radial transverse crease that travels an extended distance conjoined together with the radial arc crease reveals people who embrace good family connections.

CHARACTERISTICS

These people understand the importance of family and appreciate traditional family values. They are not impulsive in domestic matters and will do everything within their power to keep their family together. They have an inherently strong family bond. For this reason, they respect and revere previous generations. On the downside, they may be so committed to this position that they remain in unsupportive marriages or relationships.

QUALITIES

- ☾ Cautious
- ☾ Strong family values
- ☾ Conservative

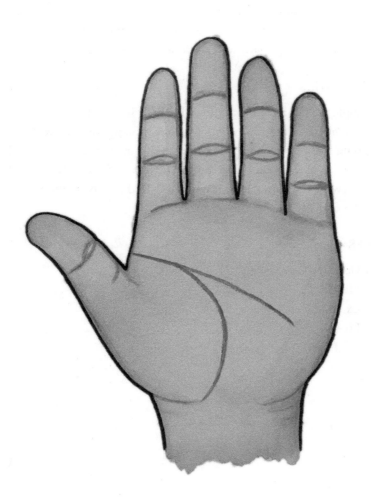

FUN-LOVING

Sometimes the middle finger will draw the upper transverse crease firmly to it. This structure attests to a robust, fun-loving spirit when around friends, and especially in an intimate relationship.

CHARACTERISTICS

These people are not afraid to ask for what they want. There's no beating around the bush; they know what they're looking for and everyone else is going to know it, too. They are emotionally charged, excited spirits. They're compatible with those who are lively, animated, and alert. Otherwise, they quickly become bored. In their darker moments, they can be demanding and self-absorbed.

QUALITIES

- Upbeat
- Playful
- Exciting
- Lively
- Bold

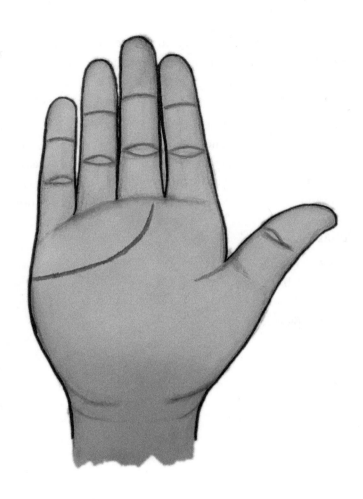

GOOD FRIEND

People who value supportive friendships will have a rounded upraised ball of the thumb (thenar region). Moreover, a large and significantly elevated thenar pad indicates an abundance of charm and sincerity.

CHARACTERISTICS

Those people who are extremely sociable and value friendships will display a full-bodied and rounded ball of the thumb. Endearing and charming, these people are able to mix business and pleasure, which is their art. On the downside, those with this feature can be impressionable and need to be more circumspect about the motivations of others.

QUALITIES

- ℂ Friendly
- ℂ Charming
- ℂ Personable
- ℂ Sincere

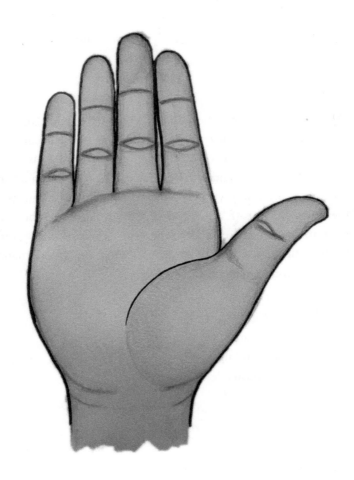

GOOD LISTENER

People whose upper transverse crease is pronounced in its length and straightness will be possessed of excellent listening skills. Make note that this line must forge a healthy incursion into the precinct beneath the index finger.

CHARACTERISTICS

These people are "emotional idealists": very supportive people who genuinely listen. As they are assured of a sympathetic ear, friends continually come to them with their feelings and problems. As they give freely of their time and energy, they can also be taken advantage of. Even if an argument ensues, they will still consider your points with the temperament of a therapist. Desiring harmony, they are always open to making shared and cooperative decisions. More importantly, those with this crease put much of their time into humanitarian or socially conscious activities.

QUALITIES

- ❮ Considerate
- ❮ Understanding
- ❮ Companionable
- ❮ Supportive

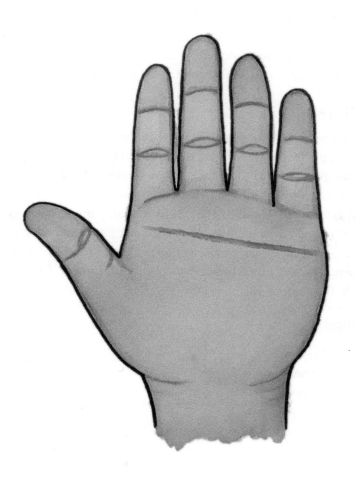

HARDWORKING

People who are responsible and hardworking by nature will have a middle finger that possesses a longer middle segment than its other two. A few vertical lines inscribed upon this section will heighten these qualities even further (possibly denoting a workaholic).

CHARACTERISTICS

This long segment shows people who are extremely self-disciplined and will apply themselves to the task at hand. They use their time efficiently as they are good at planning and organizing. They are diligent, focused, and committed. They make sure what needs to be accomplished gets accomplished. If they make a commitment, it's as good as done. They pride themselves on taking their duties and obligations seriously. Their motto is, "There is pride and honor in work." To their detriment, they are prone to sacrificing relationships with friends and family in the name of their career.

QUALITIES

- Industrious
- Conscientious
- Responsible

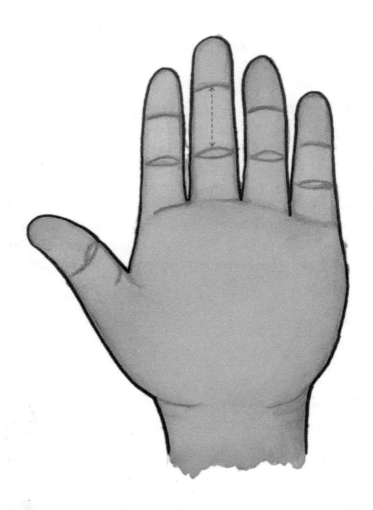

HONEST

Observe the entire length of the little finger from the back of the hand. The straighter the finger is formed, the more honest the individual.

CHARACTERISTICS

Fingers represent the mind. Therefore, straight fingers embody a straight, upright mind. Twisted fingers betray a twisted or crooked mind. The pinky is the finger of communications. When this digit is straight, communications will be straight.

Honesty is natural to those whose pinky is arrow straight. They can be trusted with your business and your money. If they miss a bill or a deadline, rest assured they'll tell you about it. They like things to be above board, and any form of deception makes them uncomfortable. Further, they are law abiding and champions of societal order and justice.

QUALITIES

     ❰   Forthright
     ❰   Scrupulous
     ❰   Upfront
     ❰   Trustworthy

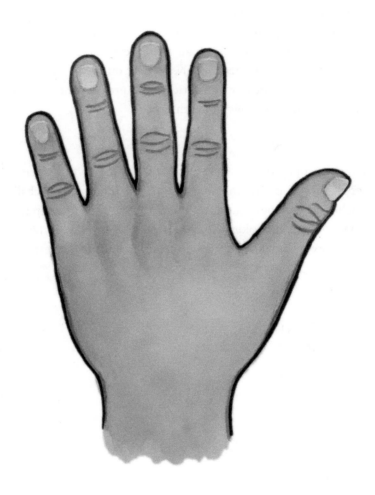

HUMOROUS

Occupying the interdigital space between the ring and little finger sits a most stimulating configuration. This fingerprint-like pattern (made up of a succession of arches within arches) evidences a great sense of humor. People with this imprint always look on the bright side of life. Further, a sharply sarcastic and critical wit is present when this pattern angle is at 45 degrees (toward the thumb).

CHARACTERISTICS

For these people, optimism springs from a quick wit. By seeing the inherent humor in life, they are able to rise above tough challenges and rebound from personal hardship. Those with this characteristic are always laughing and joking. It's also seen that those with this pattern desire a career that provides them fulfillment and creative expression.

QUALITIES

- (Funny
- (Likes to laugh
- (Witty

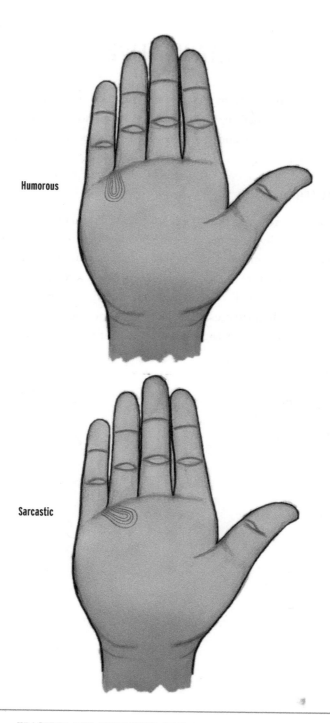

Humorous

Sarcastic

IMAGINATIVE

Notice if the medial transverse crease is etched into a curved rather than a straight formation. Owners of this formation are right-brained. Therefore, their experiences, feelings, and instincts influence their abilities and perspectives.

CHARACTERISTICS

These people are conceptually creative and imaginative. For them to be happy, their livelihood must entail some form of self-expression. Architects, musicians, and artists will own a curving medial. A crease that moves even more deeply into the hand adds a dream dimension to the mix. For instance, if they are writers, the supernatural or works of fantasy will be their themes. Also, as curving medials are right-brained, the stronger one's curve, the stronger one's intuition.

QUALITIES

- ❨ Creative
- ❨ Subjective
- ❨ Dreamy
- ❨ Intuitive

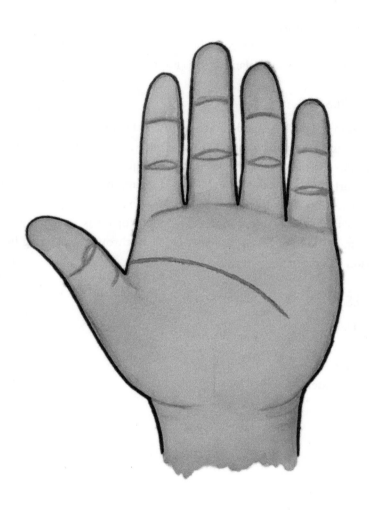

INDEPENDENT

An independent mindset is declared when the medial transverse crease begins *above* and is separated from the radial arc. Confidence and self-assurance are friendly attendants to this interspace.

CHARACTERISTICS

The freedom to take independent action and make one's own decisions is indigenous to the personality of people with this imprint. They are spontaneous and enjoy taking risks. Risks are required, as experimentation and participation, rather than observation, are the key to their success. In fact, those with this linear separation are more able to bounce back and capitalize on their failures. Starting projects is not difficult, but sustaining them is. Their difficulty is follow-through. Engaging in delegation and direction will resolve this issue.

QUALITIES

- Daring
- Assertive
- Free-thinking
- Confident

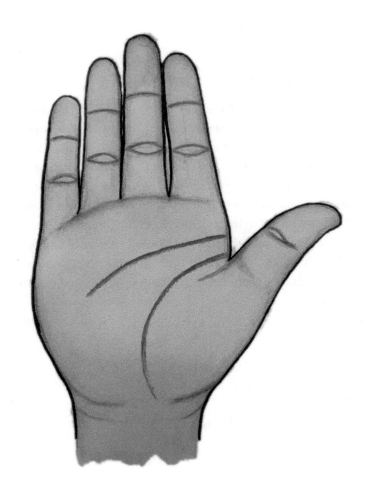

INTELLIGENT

Does the medial transverse crease extend into little finger territory? If so, this reveals people who possess a sharp, discriminating, and penetrating intelligence.

CHARACTERISTICS

These people are the eternal students. No matter their age, they are ever inquisitive. They are able to see underneath the surface of things and are the most reflective and introspective people. The ancient Egyptian adage "True knowledge is always hidden" is a way of life for them. Tomes on metaphysics, philosophy, and spirituality fill their bookshelves, and they certainly do burn the midnight oil. The phrase "Those who fail to learn from history are doomed to repeat it" is their motto, as they take the past into consideration when making decisions. They are seekers of truth and wisdom and enjoy sharing their realizations with others; therefore, writing, teaching, and counseling attract them.

QUALITIES

- ❬ Penetrating awareness
- ❬ Introspective
- ❬ Discriminating
- ❬ Discerning intelligence

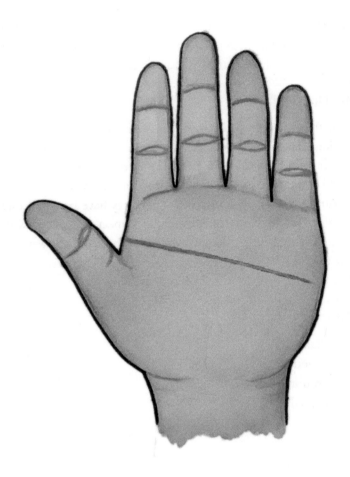

LOYAL

Although short in length, a straight upper transverse crease ending underneath the middle finger proclaims an extremely loyal nature. For these people, faithfulness is their middle name.

CHARACTERISTICS

Count on these people to be there for you—to exhibit unswerving devotion and dependability. Generally, people with this crease don't fly headfirst into love, but instead pay close attention to their partner's actions and words and wait for them to prove themselves. Once they do, they're committed for the long term. They may have trouble expressing their feelings and often need time alone. Expect them to show their love through actions rather than words, as they have difficulty articulating what they feel. They are likely to give second chances, even after being betrayed.

QUALITIES

- ☾ Reliable
- ☾ Dependable
- ☾ Committed
- ☾ Devoted

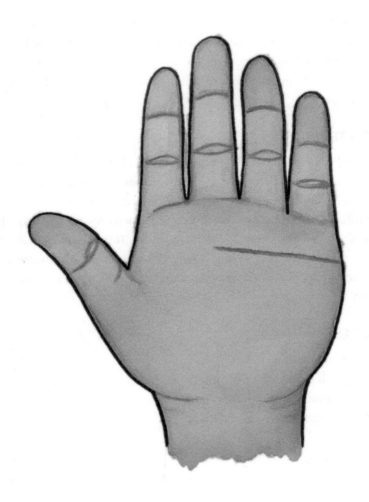

MANIPULATIVE

Formidable willpower exists when the top segment of the thumb is immoderately wide and thick. When it appears somewhat top-heavy (when compared to the rest of the thumb), a strong presence and the desire to influence their surroundings are the benchmarks of this construction.

CHARACTERISTICS

If you're looking for someone who will take charge in a relationship, this may be the person for you. People with this feature are doers; they strive for results. They are motivated to shape their environment to meet their needs. Consequently, this quality is accompanied by a strong willpower as well as drive and determination. It is the more evident, intense version of the "Strong-Willed" hand (see page 140). People with this quality may at times prove difficult to reason with and can be obstinate.

QUALITIES

- Stubborn
- High expectations of others
- Demanding
- Possessive

Standard thumb   **Egotistical thumb**

MONEYMAKING ABILITY

If the medial transverse crease draws up slightly toward the little finger as it ends its journey, it signifies a marked ability and desire to make a considerable amount of money. In addition, a spirit of competitiveness frequently accompanies this contour.

CHARACTERISTICS

These people have strong business acumen and work very hard to be successful. They seize any opportunities that come their way. They know the value of a dollar. They're efficient, resourceful, and not inclined to waste money. They'll spend money when they need to, but normally only after shopping around enough to know that they have absolutely secured the best deal. While good at managing what they have, they are always looking to increase their wealth. They make excellent investors. Therefore, this preoccupation can prove quite consuming, and they may ignore other areas of their lives, such as their health or spirituality.

QUALITIES

- Good provider
- Strong financial management
- Business ability
- Money-minded

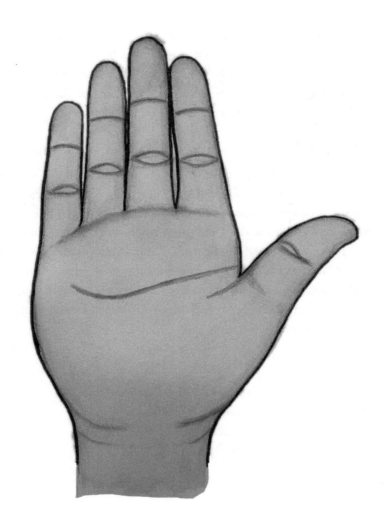

NATURE LOVER

Under a bright light, look for a skin pattern that resembles a series of arches within each other. Situated within the lower hypothenar region, it's positioned horizontally with its open side facing out, somewhat resembling a U-shaped horseshoe magnet. This marking evidences a pulling toward the great outdoors.

CHARACTERISTICS

These people can tune in to the rhythms and the cycles of nature. The ability to dowse, use a pendulum, or water-witch comes naturally, always producing successful results. They are mystically drawn to rocks and stones—and collect them wherever they go. Their disposition makes them ideal candidates for search and rescue, forest service, and wilderness training. Interestingly, those with this pattern seem to prefer mountains and forests to lakes and oceans. And, of course, their spiritual practices are best performed outdoors. At all costs, they must avoid a desk job.

QUALITIES

- The outdoorsy type
- Pronounced sense of direction
- Affinity for horticulture
- "Horse-whisperer" proclivity

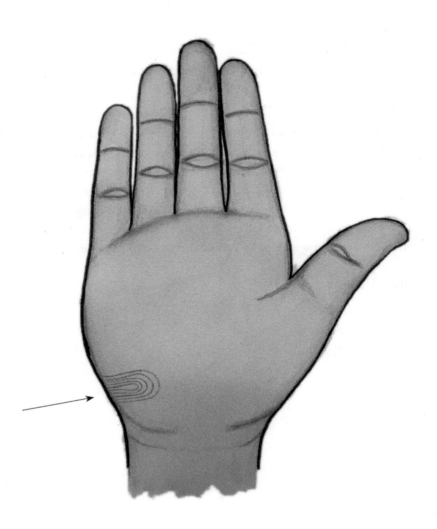

OPEN-MINDED

Looking at the relationship between the upper and middle transverse creases, observe if a fair distance exists between them at the palm's center. This is the sign of an *easygoing* mental attitude.

CHARACTERISTICS

Within relationships, people with this imprint can be quite accommodating. They are flexible, free spirits who approach life with a carefree and relaxed attitude. For them, the journey is more important than the destination. They are capable of seeing all sides of an argument, sometimes to a fault. This tendency leads them to be easily talked out of their own opinions or fail to form their own opinions at all. They should be encouraged to take a stand on important matters.

QUALITIES

- ☾ Adaptable
- ☾ Free-spirited
- ☾ Easygoing

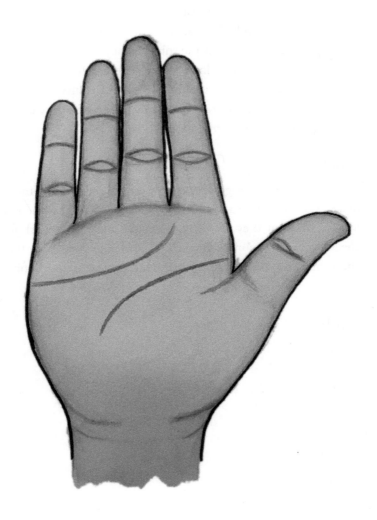

OPINIONATED

Observe the middle of the palm. Are the two major creases in close proximity to each other (a half inch apart or less)? Those who form strong personal opinions of the subjects they love will display this narrow space within their palm's center. The upper transverse crease is the current of the emotions, and the middle transverse crease is the current of the intellect. This close association of the two produces a person whose heart and mind are like one.

CHARACTERISTICS

Emotion and intellect go very deeply into every decision these people make. Therefore, they are strongly opinionated because their views are formed by what they *believe* in. They can never just work for a paycheck, but they require a career that is in alignment with their ideals and principles. All of this can make for very passionate, spirited, and strong-minded individuals.

QUALITIES

- Responsible
- Strength of character
- Independent thinker

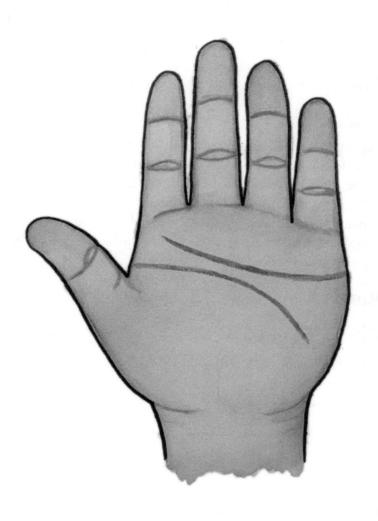

PASSIONATE

A hand in which the palm itself is slightly longer than it is square, united with fingers that are shorter than the palm, reveals people who are fervent in their hunger to gratify their wants and desires.

CHARACTERISTICS

Those with this hand are fiery and intense. They strive to create personal independence and seek a life full of challenges. It's in their nature to crave excitement and attention. However, they may be prone to abusing power and manipulating situations—sometimes our of sheer boredom! They are very good at starting projects and ventures, but not so skilled at maintaining them. They need others to manage their creations so that they can continue to create.

QUALITIES

- (Dramatic
- (Zest for life
- (Enthusiastic

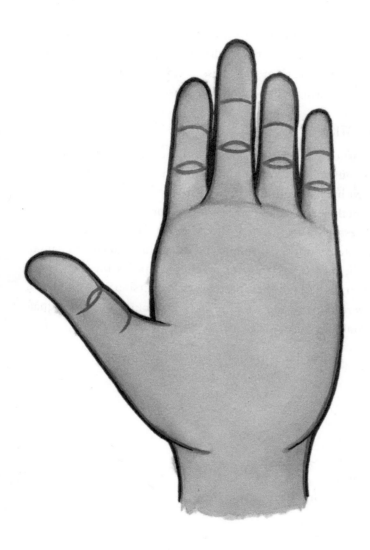

PESSIMISTIC

Note the commencement point of the medial transverse crease in relation to the radial arc crease. If the medial transverse crease begins *below*
the radial arc crease, the element of pessimism will certainly play a role
in this person's demeanor and mental outlook.

CHARACTERISTICS

Ultra-cautiousness is the modus operandi of these people. "It will never
happen." "Quit while you're ahead." Statements like this are common
for people with this imprint. Although subject to negative thinking,
they are nonetheless pragmatists who look for the bottom line and
avoid unnecessary risks. Their outlook stems from a subconscious
desire to create security and stability; they are not quick to change.
Unfortunately, they have a way of creating obstacles for themselves
and may even discourage their partners from pursuing their dreams.
Taking a few risks, being more optimistic, and thinking bigger are qualities they would do well to cultivate.

> Impossible is a word in a fool's dictionary.
> —Srila Prabhupada

QUALITIES

- (Critical
- (Judgmental
- (Cynical
- (Paranoid (in extreme cases)

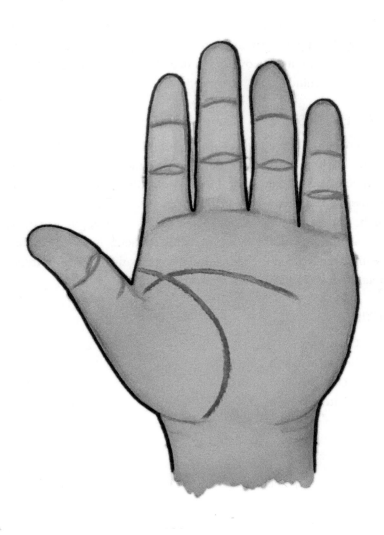

PHILOSOPHICAL

The definitive and unerring hallmark of the eternal student is proclaimed by the upper segment of the middle finger. If it is the longest of the three segments, the owner is a deep thinker and is blessed with a philosophical mind.

CHARACTERISTICS

These people are definitely not shallow thinkers. Expect individuals with this marking to be quite introspective and reflective—not just about their own lives, but about the world outside as well. They delight in discussing many subjects ranging from geo-politics to conspiracy research, from technology to sociology, and, of course, philosophy in general. An interest in the Wisdom of the Ancients is also common. These individuals are enlivened within the company of those aspirants of metaphysics and self-awareness.

QUALITIES

- Curious
- Enjoys learning
- Metaphysically minded
- Spiritual seeker

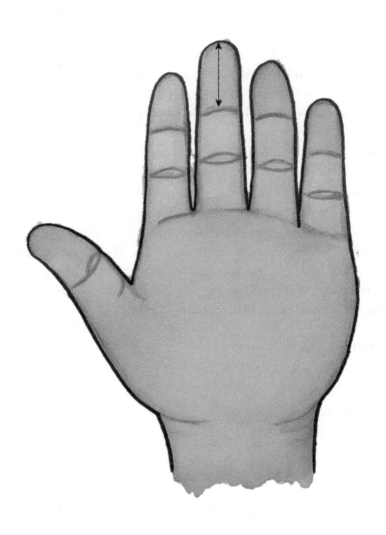

REFINED

Inspect the texture of the skin on the palm side of the hand. The degree of smoothness and softness will equal the degree of refinement and sensitivity in the temperament. Smooth, silky skin reveals a cultured, well-mannered person, while course or hard skin texture denotes a more crude disposition.

CHARACTERISTICS

Smooth texture indicates a sophisticated and sensitive nature. These are warm people who really want the best for society. It pains them to witness social degradation. They're inclined to help others elevate themselves or their immediate surroundings. These individuals will avoid places where vulgar behavior or language is found—it greatly disturbs them. They prefer to live in pleasant and attractive environments and around professional people.

QUALITIES

- Clean
- Cultured
- Polite

SELF-CENTERED

Self-centeredness is confirmed when the index finger's upper segment is the shortest of the three. If its apex is squarish, this disposition is further accentuated, and lessened if rounded.

CHARACTERISTICS

This short length is textbook confirmation of a skepticism of all things spiritual. High standards and values are lacking, as these people live in a world of moral relativism. At their worst, they are always looking out for number one, shrugging accountability and ignoring the effects of their actions on others. They do not have clearly defined viewpoints regarding what is right and what is wrong.

QUALITIES

- Selfish
- Miserly
- Ungenerous
- Insensitive

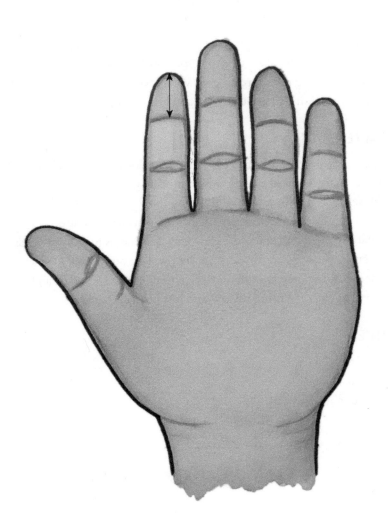

SEXUAL DRIVE

A strong sex drive is revealed by a deeply cut and dark-looking radial arc crease. This crease will also curve out spaciously. Conversely, a slightly cut and thin-looking radial crease goes with a weaker sexual desire, and the entire operation will be straighter and less curved.

CHARACTERISTICS

This line is the barometer of sexual energy. It does not, in itself, point out any tendency toward monogamy or infidelity, but a person's expression of sensuality will certainly be heightened or diminished by the quality of this line. Therefore, the degree of sensuality is directly proportionate to the depth and prominence of this line. A healthy enthusiasm to enjoy their senses, or a lust for life, will be on those who own a dark, deep, and widely curving crease. Thinner, lighter, and straighter radial arcs point out a more mental and less physical person.

QUALITIES

- Primal feelings
- Lust
- An enjoying nature

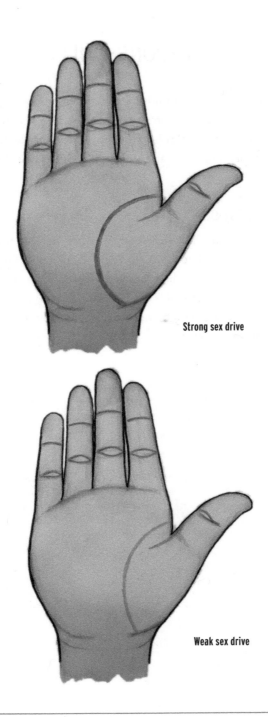

Strong sex drive

Weak sex drive

STRONG-WILLED

An enduring determination is present when a firm, well-rounded padding constitutes the thumb's upper segment. This cushion (opposite the nail side) should feel solid, resilient, and resemble the letter *D*. Similarly, if this padding is flat and feels soft, the person lacks willpower and drive.

CHARACTERISTICS

Perseverance and a healthy determination characterize these strong-willed individuals. They never give up. If a project fails, they will pull themselves up by their bootstraps and go at it again, with no loss of enthusiasm. This segment is the physical embodiment of one's strength of mind. Therefore, a segment that is soft and flat reveals that focus and concentration are weak.

QUALITIES

- (Persistence
- (Single-mindedness
- (Strong character

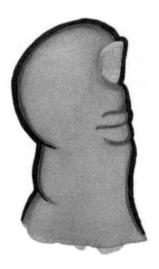

SUPERFICIAL

If the hypothenar region of the hand is flat, atrophied, or generally characterless, it denotes a superficial and unreflective mind. A pad of flesh that is slightly upraised and moderately developed by contrast would indicate an adequate contemplative ability.

CHARACTERISTICS

This feature of the hand reveals a tendency to follow the crowd and a reluctance to think critically. These are trendy people; you might say they are pop culture devotees. Their motto is, "If everyone's buying it, it's got to be good!" Their partners or friends could do them a favor by encouraging them to be more introspective—and to question ideas and behaviors before accepting them as true or beneficial.

QUALITIES

- (Shallow
- (Conformist
- (Materialistic

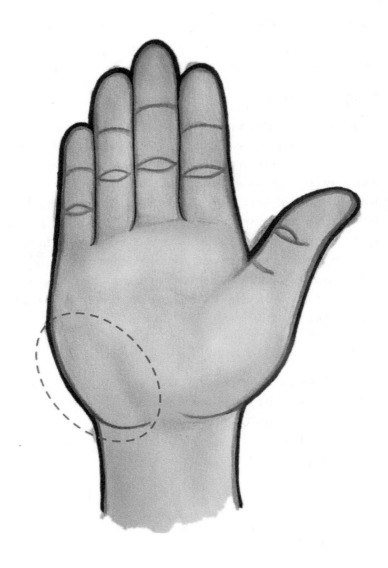

TEAM PLAYER

Here we see that the medial transverse crease travels a short distance coupled together with the radial arc. People with this marking very much enjoy collaborating with others.

CHARACTERISTICS

In the same way that the two lines begin their journey connected together, owners of this configuration love to network and work closely with others. This is the mark of someone whose actions are a good balance between cautious and risky. They take other people into account when making decisions. They are the true team players. They feel most at home in cooperative partnerships. They like to share and express their opinions while at the same time receiving feedback from others. They do require validation and acknowledgment from others, especially in business ventures. They can be self-conscious at times because they spend time worrying about what other people think about their plans and ideas.

QUALITIES

- ☾ Takes calculated risks
- ☾ Conservative in business ventures
- ☾ Enjoys interacting with colleagues
- ☾ Cautious
- ☾ Prudent

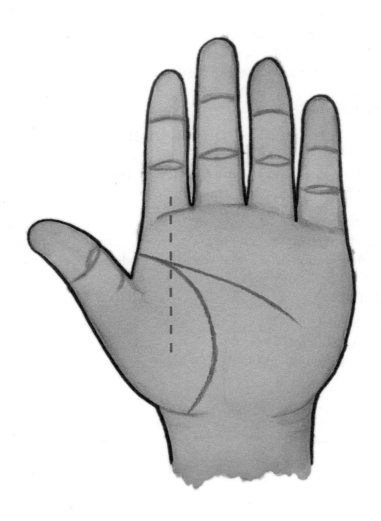

VISIONARY

Sometimes you will encounter fingertips that taper into a cone shape. Resembling the spire of a cathedral, this characteristic identifies a specific visionary prowess exclusive to the finger it appears upon.

CHARACTERISTICS

- Index Finger: Spiritual/Devotional Revelations
- Middle Finger: Mystic/Occult Powers
- Ring Finger: Paranormal/Supernatural Visions
- Little Finger: Psychic/Intuitive Insights

Make note that this "druid's hood" will be found on the same finger on both hands. Also, if three or more of these tips are in evidence, though mystically powerful, these people will lack groundedness.

QUALITIES

- Idealistic
- Inspirational
- Intuitive

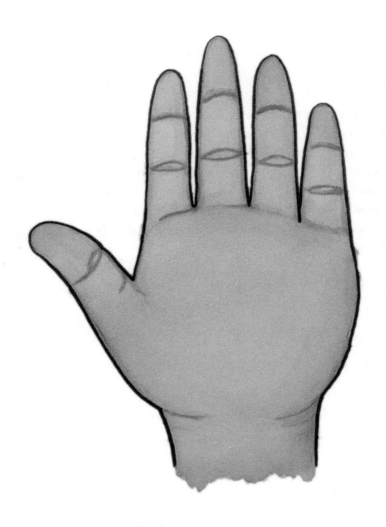

WARMHEARTED

A warmhearted nature is affirmed when the upper transverse crease ends with a gentle curve at the index finger's base.

CHARACTERISTICS

This marking identifies nurturers in relationships. They are very giving and will sacrifice their own needs to care for their partner's. It is important to understand that they crave reciprocation, too. They require to receive as much as they give, but they are shy to ask for it. They often idealize their relationships while ignoring their practical experience. Therefore, they are prone to being taken advantage of and need to ask themselves if they are honestly getting what they need out of their relationships.

QUALITIES

- (Caring
- (Codependent tendencies
- (Sharing
- (Kind

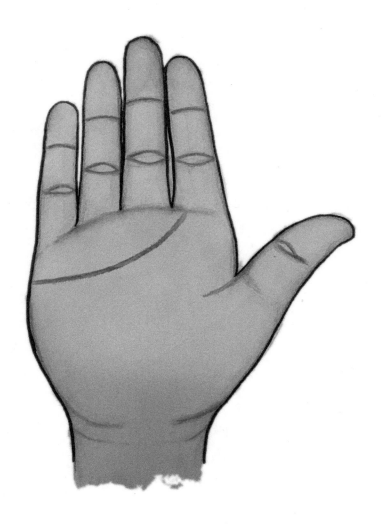

PART FOUR

FIELD NOTES OFF THE BEATEN PATH

ife presents us with formidable mental and emotional challenges. Our exploration on the palmistry trail now takes us to those areas. Owing to the indiscriminately positive New Age climate, palmistry writers consistently avoid these excursions, which take them into the realm of negative qualities and psychological dysfunction. However, in the practice of the metaphysical, unvarnished idealism is not always a virtue. With a view to broaden our vista, we will now have a look at eight of the most challenging hand topographies.

These eight qualities, on their face, may seem like normal traits, and you may ask, "Isn't everyone lazy or fickle to some degree?" The features presented in this part are those that can manifest to a particularly troubling extreme. Each entry is a potential red flag, indicating decisively debilitating or destructive consequences. Often, these features can express themselves in various forms of mental illness. For example, a conspicuously arresting example of Weakness of Mind will announce pronounced schizophrenia or bipolar disorder.

On the subject of mental illness, there is no question that it is now in epidemic proportions. In this regard, the question of the use of vaccinations is often invoked, and loud arguments are heard on both sides. As a reader of hands, I regularly confront issues of mental dysfunction, and the following sums up my thirty-plus years of research: Although our right and left brains are poles apart in function, their synergy is divine in confederation. I believe the ingredients within vaccines chemically disconnect these two lobes, severing their ability to interface and communicate. This disconnect is always in evidence in the hands of those with varying degrees of autism. Certainly, there are other environmental elements at work as well contributing to this disconnect. Nevertheless, my ability as a Seer equips me with a uniquely powerful entrance into the deepest provinces of the human mechanism, and I am convinced without a doubt that they are a contributing factor.

MERCURIAL OR VOLATILE

The upper transverse crease registers the qualities and character of one's emotions and feelings. It is the foremost indicator within the hand of the manner in which a person will relate to others.

The healthy formation of this line is one that is straight across with an occasional gentle upward curve in the direction of the index finger. This marking indicates an emotional psychology that is able to be resolute in affections and attachments.

However, if this crease is wavering in its course, the bearer's emotions are constantly changing and fluctuating. In relationships, these people will run hot and cold—completely in love one day and entirely detached the next. Thus, their feelings are unpredictable and extremely fickle. In their everyday affairs, they lack the needed staying power and endurance to achieve results. When they are required to make choices, their vacillating heart leads them to be indecisive and hesitating.

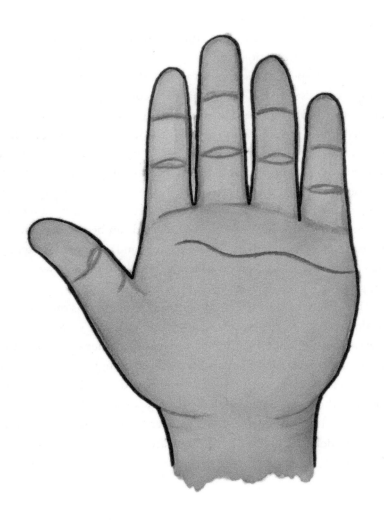

SLOTH

The physical consistency of the hands is a mirror of one's body and mind. Hands that feel firm and sturdy exhibit a personality imbued with energy, determination, and benefic (vibrant) health. Softer hands, in comparison, speak of lesser motivation and weaker physical reserves.

One will also find that hard hands accompany a hard temperament, while soft hands belong to one with a softer disposition. It is not uncommon to find a pair of hands that are so exceeding in their softness that they have the look and feel of a marshmallow. As these hands resemble a plushy pillow, their ideal is a life reveling in comfort and ease. Cushioned palms prefer a cushy life. Lazy and lethargic, they prefer to have others pamper them, indulge them, and carry things out for them. They love rich, luxurious foods and can be undisciplined in their eating. Consequently, poor eating habits and a distaste for exercise make them sluggish and procrastinating, unable to push forward with their goals.

The texture of the skin on the surface of the palm is the gauge of one's receptivity to the world. Coarse skin, as found on solid hands, shows an overall limited sensitivity, whereas smoother skin indicates a high level of affectability. Skin quality on these spongy hands is without exception so smooth as to be almost satiny and silky in composition. This gives the bearer such a high degree of sensitivity that coping with the real world is formidable. Further, over-emotionalism, hypersensitivity, and delicate, easily hurt feelings are attributes associated with this velvety textured skin.

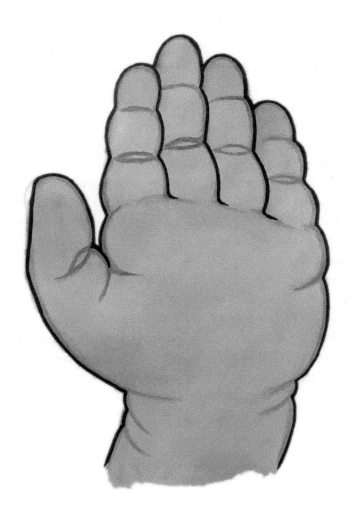

LACK OF SELF-CONFIDENCE

The index and ring fingers are typically the same length, either one likely to be only a centimeter or two taller than the other. However, the index is considered short if it scarcely reaches the middle finger's upper demarcation line. Consequently, the ring finger will look noticeably longer in comparison.

The index symbolizes an "I can" spirit and bestows the needed amount of confidence and courage to take on the world.

When the index finger is short, the bearer is unceasingly plagued by self-doubt and feelings of insufficiency. These people act helpless and overwhelmed due to being quite intimidated by the outer world. Even if there is an inherent desire to impact their environment, they are unable to take advantage of this because they lack confrontational skills and assertive ability.

In relationships, these people give their power away by not standing up for themselves. Thus, they are easily influenced and taken advantage of, always playing a subordinate role. Their low self-image and feelings of insecurity explain their mentality of stuckness and self-limitation. Paralyzed by fear of failure and inferiority, they play the role of the professional victim. If they want to move forward in life, "What the mind can conceive, one can achieve" must be their daily mantra.

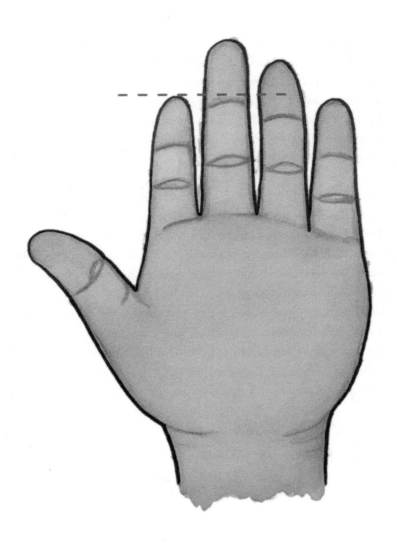

ANGER

The middle transverse crease has its start at the thumb side of the palm. It customarily begins attached to or slightly above the radial arc crease. A sufficient level of optimism and hopefulness is a fundamental aspect of the personality of people with these starting points. However, if this line begins within the Mars domain (and consequently below the radial arc), a formidable quantity of anger is intrinsically rooted to the interior of the consciousness.

The owners of this contour are essentially pessimists. They are suspicious of people's motives, and their negative thinking makes them distrustful of others. In ordinary conversation, they easily fall into feeling that they are being put on the defensive or that they are being attacked. Their habitual reaction is to take a hostile or aggressive approach. They can be sharply critical or harshly sarcastic in speech. They may also be overly paranoid.

Subconsciously, they have major issues regarding freedom, and when their independence is thwarted, anger and rage are the result. At their worst, they can be violent. This configuration is the mark of the victim who blames society for their difficulties. These are the people least able to understand that they are the architects of their own destiny.

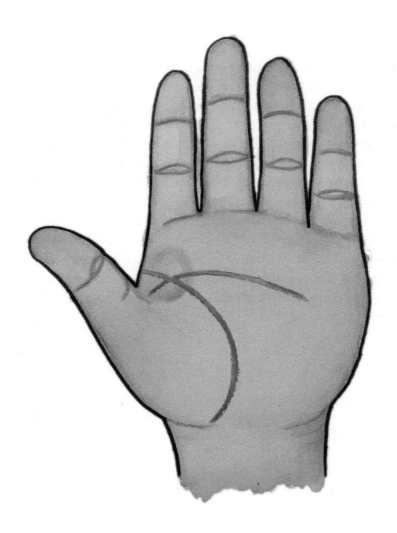

GLUTTONY

Each of the four fingers is made up of three segments that vary in length and width. They are all generally proportionate to each other and, as a set, the lower sections are usually wider by a shade.

It is not uncommon, however, to find these lower sections inordinately fat and protuberant, thus appearing very out of character with the rest of the finger sections. The standard development of these lower divisions indicates that these people feel adequate contentment from moderate sensual gratification. However, these overly swelled segments emblematize a consistent shortfall of satiation—thus, inciting a ceaseless struggle with excessive weight gain.

The origin of this overindulgence is due to harboring very deep-rooted emotional insecurities based on issues of survival. Without understanding that their actual hunger is for secure foundations and stability, these people nevertheless try to satisfy their need for security by food and other sensual gratifications. Consequently, their appetites always remain unfulfilled.

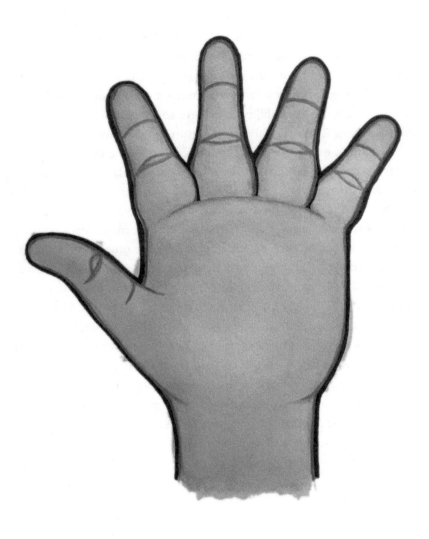

EGOTISTICAL

The upper segment of the thumb is the storehouse of willpower and determination. It represents the ability to create and shape one's environment. In its customary and natural structure, it will have perpendicular edges that border the nail and gently taper to a conical apex. A desirable level of perseverance and motivation is available with this contour—providing the ability to achieve solid results. Moreover, the ability to know when to yield is also a feature affiliated with this pattern.

Thumbs are occasionally encountered that have edges that are so wide and rounded out as to remind one of a spatula. This expansion symbolizes too much of a good thing—and a desire to impact becomes a desire to dominate. These swelled thumbs physically personify a swelled ego. Aspiring to take charge and control their surroundings, these people can be very demanding and expect others to do things exactly their way. They are quite difficult to reason with once they have determined their agendas, and will be forceful and obstinate in carrying them out. This type of thumb attests to a fervent attachment to their business and social positions, as well as to their accomplishments. Loved ones and colleagues are seen almost as possessions.

On a psychological level, owners of these thumbs believe strongly that opportunities only present themselves if they aggressively pursue them. They do not accept the viewpoint that gain can come of its own accord or by the goodwill of Providence. "Let go and let God" is never their ideology, and patience and humility are rarely found in them.

WEAKNESS OF MIND

The middle of the palm is home to a horizontal line known as the medial transverse crease. This crease is the window to the mind. Sometimes called the seventh chakra, it is a barometer of one's power of concentration. A deeply engraved and well-defined crease reveals an able capability to conceive a plan and follow it through until completion. A respectable memory, a marked attention span, and a capacity for introspection are also the hallmarks of a rich and deeply etched line.

Unfortunately, this crease is sometimes found in a substantially weakened condition. A clean and continuous line testifies to mental and psychological harmony, while a feeble and fragmentary crease points out psychic discord. The inability to focus attention due to scattered and disorganized thought processing accompanies a thin and lightly cut line. This is the mark of people who are easily distracted and indecisive. Sometimes along its journey, parts of the line will form into elongated bubbles. These are a sign that the person suffers from continuous mental tension and strain. This crease can be so badly constructed that instead of carving one continuous path, it will be composed of many broken intermittent fragments. In this case, acute psychological disturbances and various mental complexes are constitutionally ingrained within the consciousness. Occasional low moods and periods of sadness are an unavoidable element of life. However, mood swings, despondencies, and depressions are far more pronounced for owners of an unsound medial crease.

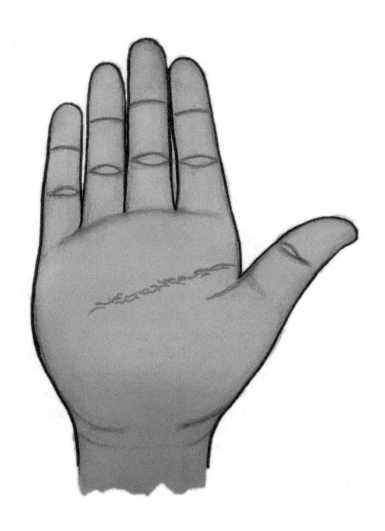

CRIMINALITY

Like the stumps of a tree, the lower segments of the fingers are usually broader and wider than the two atop them. They are also more or less the same length or longer than the upper segments. As a set, these lower four segments are the physical embodiment of a psychological and instinctual craving for strong material foundations. As repositories of the attributes of caution and prudence, these lowers infuse these qualities into the subconscious mind. Those with strongly developed sections dislike change and are conservative with their money and career. Not surprisingly, these sections are usually found to be the most sturdy and substantial within Western culture.

Pairs of hands are found in which these segments are conspicuously shorter than that of their counterparts. Those with this structure are short on forethoughtfulness, which in their case is replaced with a psychology of heedless impulsiveness. With this lack of inner stability and groundedness to temper one's desires, a "to hell with the consequences" attitude prevails. Consequently, this is the hand of the career criminal, sex offender, murderer, or serial killer.

Make note that these segments will not only look short, but in some cases will also even taper in at their base or midpoint. The fingers will then resemble trees that are in the first stages of being cut down, causing them to appear top-heavy and unstable. This modification adds additional instability and insecurity to the mentality.

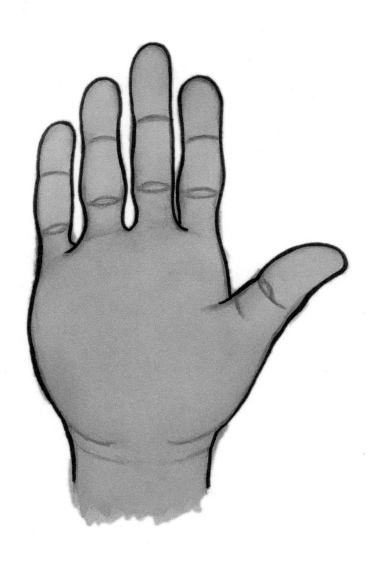

CONCLUSION

For thousands of years, astronomers *were* astrologers. They were in full concurrence of the interrelationship between planetary rotation and human destiny. This percipience unfortunately ended with the age of reason. Today's scientists accept terrestrial influences (such as gravity) but roundly dismiss forces more dynamic—the celestial. As astronomy split off into the realm of real and scientific, astrology was relegated to the domain of the unreal and mystical. And so mankind, as well, started to split into two—body separate from soul and psyche. Nevertheless, it's now common to accept the full moon's affectivity over the human psyche; it's well documented that human behavior changes during the full moon, for example. Even the term *Mercury retrograde*—a three-week period in which communication glitches abound—is now becoming mainstream.

Our spiritual soul resides within the physical heart. This spirit spark is encased in not just one, but two earthly bodies: the corporeal body, of blood and bone, and the subtle body of mind and intelligence. The ancient Egyptians referred to them as the *Ka* and the *Ba*. The planets emit their own type of Wi-Fi, and the subtle body is the receiver. The subtle body then transfers this planetary data to the soul, which in turn imprints it onto the palm. Therefore, the hand is a living astrological chart—a clear roadmap to our successful destinations. Most amazing is that this entire map is fully carved into the palms of the unborn child at seven months in the womb!

Instilling fortitude and independence by identifying strengths and weaknesses is the beauty of hand analysis. That not withstanding, to aid in the progressive advancement of God-consciousness is palmistry's

greatest treasure. To detach from mammon and attach to devotion; endeavoring to free the soul from the bondage of materialism. The question may then be raised: if the configurations on the hand are a result of planetary influence (karma), are there markings on the hands of the saintly? Yes! The palms of the great devotees of the Lord evidence stunning symbolism, but they are carved directly by the soul, and not by the brain. They are markings of liberation and love—not of limitation and lust.

The soul continually whispers, lifetime after lifetime, through the heart, and through the hand, to begin one's real journey—the Spiritual Journey. To go back home, back to Godhead.

Hare Krishna Hare Krishna Krishna Krishna Hare Hare
Hare Rama Hare Rama Rama Rama Hare Hare

ACKNOWLEDGMENTS

SPIRITUAL INSPIRATIONS

Srila Bhaktivedanta Narayana Gosvami Maharaja • Srila Bhaktivedanta Swami Maharaja Prabhupada • Srila Bhakti Vaibhava Puri Gosvami • Srila Bhakti Rakshak Shridhara Gosvami • Srila Bhakti Prajnana Keshava Gosvami • Srila Bhaktisiddhanta Sarasvati Thakur Prabhupada • Srila Saccidananda Bhativinoda Thakur

FAMILY AND FRIENDS

Kanhaiya Enki Mahabal • Jahnava Chan-Edwards • Syamala • Tirthapada • Gopinatha • Pran Kishore. Champakalata • Chiranjib • Shamapriya. Catur Vyuha • Bhumipati • Sahadeva • Carrie Butterworth • Anupama. Malati Rossington. • Madhu • Rom Roy • Atulananda • Todd Youth • Madhumangala (Mike) • Kenny Murtagh • Dina Bandhu • Jonathan Glass • Sivananda Sena • Krsna Mayi • John Mini • Dan Glenn. Jill Tabler. Radhanath • Kalimba • Dominque Edgerly • Christian Avery • Chris and Lon Staub • Mark Koperweis • Jennifer Yeager • Dr. Michael Savage • Lisa Lyon • George Noory • and the most awesome agent in the world, Peter Giagni

ESTEEMED PALMISTS AND ASTROLOGERS

Alana and Richard Unger • Kay Packard • Karen Page • Amber Flynn • Padabja • Michael Geary • Spencer Grendahl • Ghanshyam Birla • Johnny Fincham • Andrew Fitzherbert • J. Owen Swift • William Benham

INSPIRATIONS

Alexander Solzhenitsyn • Fyodor Dostoyevsky • Jules Verne • Ludwig Van Beethoven • Black Sabbath • Iron Maiden • Judas Priest • Trouble • Ramones • Celtic Frost • Nile • King Diamond • Slayer • Ronnie James Dio • Sleep • Jean-Luc Ponty

ABOUT THE AUTHOR

Vernon Mahabal is the founder and director of the Palmistry Institute in Los Angeles, California. The objectives of the Palmistry Institute are to further new advances in the field of hand analysis and to serve as a research and information resource. In 1979 he began formal training in Vedic (Eastern) cosmology, which took him to India many times. He combines both Eastern and Western astrological disciplines into his practice. He also continues new research, particularly within the field of dermatoglyphics (fingerprint biometrics).

Vernon is the bestselling author of *The Secret Code on Your Hands*, *The Palmistry Cards*, and *Crossing Paths*. He has written articles for *Women's Day* magazine, *First for Women*, and the *New York Daily News*. He is the palmistry consultant for *Coast To Coast AM*, is the palmist to Dr. Michael Savage (The Savage Nation radio talk show), and has also been consulted by the New York Police Department. Mahabal has read thousands of hands, given hundreds of lectures, and trained hundreds of students. His institute serves to restore the Art of Palmistry to its previous dignity as a respected and esteemed science. He can be reached at *palmistryinstitute.com*

TO OUR READERS